(Un)bound
Five Years of Asterisms

More Aster(ix) Anthologies

Edges
Fall 2018

Dirty Laundry
Fall 2017

Kitchen Table Translation
Summer 2017

Best of Kweli
Spring 2017

What We Love
Fall 2016

Atravesando
Spring 2016

available for order wherever books are sold

Aster(ix) Journal

presents

(Un)bound

Winter 2018/2019

***

Edited by
Angie Cruz & Adriana E. Ramírez

BLUE SKETCH PRESS | PITTSBURGH

See page 199 for individual copyright information/acknowledgments.

Published via Blue Sketch Press, Pittsburgh.
www.bluesketchpress.com

(Un)bound: Five Years of Asterisms
An Aster(ix) Anthology / Aster(ix) Journal
Edited by Angie Cruz and Adriana E. Ramírez—1st ed.
ISBN (print) 978-1-942547-10-5 (trade paperback)
1-942547-10-5 (ISBN-10)
Cover art by Evie Shaffer, on Instagram at @evieshaffer, and artwork available at https://unsplash.com/@evieshaffer
Cover Design by Little Owl Creative.
Copy-Edited by Joseph N. Welch III.

First Edition: December 2018

Printed in the United States of America
9 8 7 6 5 4 3 2 1

Aster(ix) Journal

www.asterixjournal.com

Aster(ix) is usually published 2-3 times a year in print with additional content online. **Aster(ix)** is funded in part by the Dietrich School of Arts and Sciences and the Department of English at University of Pittsburgh.

Contents

A Conversation
Angie Cruz, Patricia Engel, Stephanie Elizondo Griest, Nelly Rosario and Marissa Johnson-Valenzuela 13

Two Poems
Leslieann Hobayan 22

Once More, with Feelings
Mahwash Shoaib 26

Autumn Lessons by F. Marzia Esposito
fiction translated by Jeanne Bonner 28

My Big Gay Essay
Carley Moore 41

"What is the Difference between Globalization and Neoliberalism?"
Amy Sara Carroll 56

Two Poems
Rosamond S. King 58

Firelei Báez on Generosity and Freedom in Art
Angie Cruz 60

Bamboo Wedding
fiction by Sujatha Fernandes 78

What We Know About Men
Isobel O'Hare 99

Two Poems
Rina Garcia Chua 106

Native Tongue
Ola Osifo Osaze 111

Preferences
fiction by Amina Gautier 125

Lost the Root
Isabel Acevedo 130

The World We Choose, the World We Love
Michelle Yasmine Valladares 131

Dao Strom in Conversation
Vi Khi Nao 134

Powder Puff
fiction by Estella Gonzalez 148

La Llorona at the Saloon
José Angel Araguz 160

The Chemist's Wife
Em Rose 162

How to be Courageous: Llanto Mundo
Angie Cruz 167

Tal'-s-Go Gal'-Quo-Gi Di-Ded'-Qua-S-Do-Di Tsa-La-Gi Di-Go-Whe-Li / Beginning Cherokee
Qwo-Li Driskill 178

Contributors 187
Acknowledgments 199

A Conversation

On *Aster(ix)*, Five Years Later

Adapted from the AWP Panel, "Aster(ix) Five Year Later, A Conversation with Angie Cruz, Patricia Engel, Stephanie Elizondo Griest, Nelly Rosario and Marissa Johnson Valenzuela."

In 2013 when we started *Aster(ix),* we didn't know what we were committing ourselves to, but for the past five years the journal has been fueled with urgency, love and desire for a space that could house our wild tongue, imagination and vision.

The conceptual workings, the collective drive, the roots of *Aster(ix)* were born in 1997 when Marta Lucía Vargas, Adelina Anthony and I built WILL: Women in LIterature and Letters, a collective of women writers of color committed to social justice and community. Back then many of us were just starting out, unpublished, some of us the lone POC in our MFA programs. Many of these women from WILL are now on the *Aster(ix)* masthead and are contributors to the journal.

So for five years now alongside co-founder Adriana E. Ramírez, *Aster(ix)* continues to be shaped and reshaped through ongoing conversations and questions we ask of ourselves but also of each other. This conversation at AWP centered around the questions: Why do this work? Who is responsible for our work? What does a space where we can be our true selves look like? How can we mind meld, heart meld, spirit meld our bodies, and resources toward our collective goals? Is it possible to have a space of literary freedom?

—Angie Cruz

Angie Cruz: I would like to jumpstart this conversation sharing some of your needs and urgencies as writers at this moment and what are some of the things that excite you in this contemporary moment. I am also wondering if any of you have ideas on possible transformative spaces for WOC/artists and writers?

Nelly Rosario: I'm thinking about silence and about visibility. About the need for space and silence to work. At the same time, lack of visibility creates a vacuum. People ask about new work, especially when there are not too many of us represented in literature. Can we afford to stay in the cave? There's always the tension of coexisting between the inside and the outside worlds. Between practicing the profession and staying in the field. The professionalization of identity, another question. Being asked to anthropologize the writing process, although I'm interested in all kinds of things.

Stephanie Elizondo Griest: Last night, I was reading an issue of *Aster(ix)* and found the conversation with Sandra Cisneros where Angie mentioned how a lot of writers of color have a challenge placing their work. Especially when their work is not performing their identity politics. She also mentioned a tendency for women of color not to submit their work at all. I actually do submit work regularly--a ton of work, especially to one prominent magazine that shall remain nameless. I have queried them twelve times in the last decade, and when I say query, I mean that I write a lengthy, detailed proposal that took months of research.

For ten years now, I've been writing all sorts of journalistic stories about two communities in particular: Chicanos and Native Americans. Every single time I would send the editor one of my pitches, he would write back and say, "Great story, too local." For ten years. "Great story, too local." There's actually something wonderfully woke about his response: like, we are spirits all around us kind of local. But I don't think that's what he meant. And simultaneous with that, the response I would get from secondary publications was always: "Great story, too depressing." So that's what I think is so special about *Aster(ix)*. We are our own kind of local! We don't have to explain ourselves. We can just be.

AC: One of the things I struggle with is work-life balance. Finding time for people I love, doing the work I want to do, doing my own creative writing, but feeling an urgency to do more, like this is not enough. And I'm thinking about the conversation Stephanie mentions with Sandra Cisneros that we published in our Fall 2018, issue, *Dirty Laundry*, and one of the things she talks about is how she felt this need to rescue because she was given this gift, this bestseller that everyone was reading, and in return she wanted to give back. And how the demand of the organization's work affected her writing time. So she pulled away from that work to focus on her creativity. But of course I was like if not us then who will do the work. Work, like we are trying to do for *Aster(ix)*. How do we find a way, like Nelly was saying, to do the work in the field versus the work of being public, the demand of being public when we are one of the few Latinx writers with published books. I wonder how you all continue to negotiate this—Marissa can you speak to your commitment to teaching, working in prisons while trying to finish your book.

Marissa Johnson-Valenzuela: I teach at community college full-time. I have ninety-eight students. I love my students, but it's a lot of work. During Spring Break this year, I was in prison. I was teaching a creative writing class. The men there were like, what are you doing here? They were questioning my motives. And I agreed, but not in the way I think they meant. Who am I? What am I doing here? This is my spring break. I could be on a beach right now. And they were like, woah, you're going too far. We laughed. It made me think about how maybe there is something wrong with me.

And I probably do need to find more of a balance. We're living in what feels like the worst horror telenovela. The thing I find myself urgently needing more than ever is joy. Imagination and alternatives. Now we're seeing through everything. More people than ever are realizing, oh, capitalism really is dependent on our misery—what else is possible? And I think that is something that writers and artists offer: alternative paths. But what I look to and what I'm hoping for is joy. Admittedly, I find a lot of joy in pretty sad shit (prison), but it's not all that.

I think offering an alternative vision of how to be with each other, that's the type of thing *Aster(ix)*, and small presses and independent weirdo things do really well. It's offering other narratives and a space to be ourselves. They're not neat little packages. So going back to this idea of seeing folks who look like you or have your narrative: how important that is. Because it helps you imagine something else for yourself. And imagine something else for everyone. The book I have next to me here is tied to the novel I'm writing, it's a collection of Zapatista speeches and one of the things that stuck out when I was going through it recently was how it's much easier to die than to live. And so, what can living look like?

AC: I feel like all of us are struggling with how to manage our time so we can do all the things, especially our creative work. Maybe we can give each other ideas on how to create a life where we can continue our commitment to our communities and do the work?

Patrica Engel: In my case, I think I sort of figured out that in finding balance, there's no balance. It's never going to happen. And basically my whole life is just shifting the balance so that things can get done.

AC: How do you do that?

PE: With sacrifices. There are times when everything will get neglected just so I can write and actually get something done. Meaning, I won't go out, I won't see friends, people close to me will feel my isolation, my physical activity will suffer, my nutrition. Everything will suffer except the writing. And the work will be good. And then there are other times when my personal life is flourishing and everyone around me is happy because I'm present, but I'm not getting any writing done. Teaching is also a big timesuck. I used to always ask more experienced writers, how do you do it? And sometimes I would get really hostile answers. They would be like, "You just deal with it!" But now I realize in my case, once I stop asking that question, then I don't have that anxiety anymore. It's just a constant shifting of things to make the space. And that's okay. It's okay. You don't have to be operating at maximum capacity, one hundred percent productivity, all the time, in every way. Life happens, and you know, you have to let life happen, and then there are times when art happens, and you gotta make room for that too.

SEG: I made a choice a long time ago that writing was the endeavor that I would pursue in this lifetime, and I have not strayed from that. All I wanted was to travel and to write about those travels and the people I encountered during those travels. I never bought a house or acquired children or pets or plants. I was nomadic for many years and lived in several different countries. This is my path. And for many years, I doubted this path nearly every second of the way.

Then last September, I got diagnosed with ovarian cancer, a cancer that many women die from. Once I recovered from the shock of the diagnosis, I felt a galactic shot of euphoria. Turns out, I had made the right decision after all. I was so grateful that I had spent so much time writing books, because they are now out in the world, and would continue to be so, even if I wasn't. I realized that if everything ended, I would have no regrets. I had lived the life I wanted to live. I was out in the world, I was meeting people, I was writing, I was speaking, I was activating, I was being inspired at every turn. That in and of itself became a life well lived. So if you think this is your path too, trust it. You are drawn to it for a reason. Don't second guess yourself. Go for it..

NR: I've learned a lot about slowing down from my parents. My mother slow-cooks, we talk. Then we got her an iPad, and it was funny to watch her on it. Just incongruent, you know--she's, like, slapping it, doesn't understand windows, the typical age disconnect. Giving her this new kind of time--screen time-- made me feel a little guilty. I mean, now she can watch her Dominican talk shows and international dramas, do her word searches and read recipes, so it's great. But now we all sit with our screens, in separate but connected spheres of time. We speak faster, interrupt thoughts...So yeah, I've been thinking a lot about our shifting relationship to time and its relationship to isolation, how much more aware of it I am when alone in my apartment. Someone actually referred to me as a "reclusive writer," which made me cringe. Reclusive as in creepy man who lives in the woods? Or as in I'm not posting on Facebook all the time? But reclusive is what many of us have become.

I'm trying to turn away from screens, ignoring my phone, writing by hand, going by the river to write. This slowing down slows down clocks at every scale, on and off the page. Magical things happen physically to the story on the page that I somehow miss onscreen. What I'm feeling, dreaming, being gets encoded in the body, then onto the page. A snake once appeared to me at the river, and I put that in the story. All kinds of stuff has happened while I'm there, at water's edge. So I think the only way to manage time is to not manage it so hard, slow it down. This is the only solution I have, because this whole thing about perfection and trying to do everything, I just can't. It causes too much stress. I'm not interested in breadth, I'm interested in depth. And I don't want to create shallow work that is everywhere. What does all this mean geometrically? What does this all mean in terms of vertical distance? I take a lot of walks. The story starts moving from the body.

MJV: For me, it's about trying to cut things out. Recently I was hanging out with Justin Torres and Zinzi Clemmons and they stopped me and said, *Marissa, you do a lot of things, you need to stop and step away. You need to finish this book. We need you.* And that's why I want to say their names. We are friends but not super close friends. It was like, *oh you see me and you're right.* It's hard, because for me, my writing comes out of those spaces. And teaching and organizing are also things I'm good at. I became a poet, in part, because I wasn't good at working on the book during the semester. Many of my students are high-need, and they're amazing, but it doesn't leave a lot of space and energy for writing a novel. Before that, I did social work, and the last thing you want to do after a day of working with the poorest people in Philadelphia is keep writing your book. I mean, I'm lucky I didn't develop a drinking problem to be honest.

Anyway, the point being is balancing and honoring the writing as well. And being able to look at the big picture. So this summer, I'm not going to teach in the summer for the first time ever. And just be broke, and try to make space and take that space. Finish this book. Work life balance is a constant negotiation, but I wouldn't be the writer I want to be if I stopped doing all the other things. And then I need to try not to worry that we are probably going to go on strike.

AC: I think there's the idea that if we're not out there, like in social media for example, we're outside the conversation. If we are not moving fast or writing things that can be taken in quickly we are less relevant, but for me writing is really slow. Maybe that's true for all of us, our book projects, our research, etc.. And I do think that there are ways we can shut everything out and make time for the work but circling back to what Nelly said at the beginning of this conversation what is the cost of being in the field? What are people's expectation? Why should we care?

Many years ago I was hosting Maxine Hong Kingston for an event. My son was two and I couldn't find a babysitter! And I was freaking out because I wanted to be there with her. And she said, go be with your son. You don't have to be here with me. You could read my book. And I was like, *what do you mean?! You're Maxine Hong Kingston! I don't want to miss out on what you're going to say*. And she was like, *I made that same mistake when I was your age. I had a kid, and I would give him marshmallow bags to keep him busy so I could finish my book.*

She goes, *I'm still writing books. But I missed him. I wasn't present. And now, he doesn't want to hang out with me! He has other people. I missed that experience.*

So I guess this all goes with what you all have been saying in different ways, about living your life the way you want to live it. Whatever you decide to do: be a parent, be a writer, it's all good. To forgive yourself for not being or doing everything. I think it's a major thing. It's impossible to do everything really well at the same time. But you could do things well if you parcel it out. And how important it is to create a community that supports you. And being that we are all here to support *Aster(ix)* and to think about why or if we should be doing this work, I want to thank you for supporting the journal and the space we are trying to create, a space that has an elasticity for play. And also for missing deadlines. Happy Five Years!

All I Want Is You

Leslieann Hobayan

a golden shovel
after U2

Junior year, I fell into you,
roped in by this song. We say
how we feel with others' voices. You
knew this, but lied about your want
of me, led me to a highway of diamonds
that vanished in the night on
the tailwind of a trailer, a
Mac truck in the desert. My body ring-
ing at your touch, a brush of
fingertips on lips. I was drawn to the gold
in your eyes, the glitter of your
laugh, seduced by a spun story,
a gleaming set-up for you to
push my head between your legs, remain
there in darkness, your intent untold,
tucked into the folds of your
boxers. You tried to sell this as love:

your dick in my mouth, not
the scrawled poems I wanted to
cup in my hands, with which to grow
a glow between us despite a cold
tempest of gravel. A desk lamp was all
the light we had. I thought it enough for the
sparks I started: glimmered promises
of devotion, sweet kisses. But we
were not we. The lamp's bulb break-
ing into daylight, stale beer from
red cups on your shelf cleared the
fog within me. The cradle
of your hands on my head changed to
a vice from which I broke free. The
song now ruined, buried in the grave-
yard of my heart, when
I only sought shine to cast out all
shadow from my dark corners. I
stood up, walked out, shook off my want
of you. But the damage was done. This is
the song's serrated edge, sharpened by you.

Dear Home,

Leslieann Hobayan

Capiz shell windows. Jeepneys. The sea.

White house, red shutters. Sunburst Lane bursting with sun. Dirt bikes and skinned knees,
the white boy who held my hand, loved me at nine.

Pancit and lumpia. Lechon and kare-kare. Baptisms, communions, first place math team.
Basketball in driveways and A Tribe Called Quest. Line dancing and cotillions. Tinikling and
karaoke.

Have you been swept out to sea by Typhoon Haiyan, brushed away with Samar, Lolo's
hometown, like crumbs off a table, the rugged sound of Visaya buried in water?

Or dissolved into the memories of elders who have forgotten how to speak?

Have you run away from this girl bursting with sun? Does the touch of my hand singe?

Perhaps you are my children's laughter sprinkled over tea parties. A full spread of plastic
cakes and My Little Ponies. Tiny cups of hot chocolate. The snow outside whipping against
the window.

Maybe you are the sound of a church choir singing "Be Not Afraid," voices echoing in the
rafters. The Body of Christ melting on my tongue.

Perhaps you are the taste of Om in my mouth.

Though Sherlin is not a lane of sunburst, the shine still slides along driveways staccatoed by
basketballs and rim shots. The smell of damp leaves and charred husks of grilled corn.
Adobo slowly cooking on the stove.

But maybe not.

Perhaps you have been right here all along, deep in my belly: a fire.

Once More, with Feelings

Mahwash Shoaib

let us give thanks this eid
for the thirst
of the first gulp of water that expanded like mercy in our ribs
the morsels of dates that coated our teeth with tenderness
the wedges of citrus that refreshed our senses

let us give thanks this eid
to the generous chickpea in all its guises

let us give thanks this eid
for the hunger
that cleansed us of the weight of sodium and sugar
the fried snacks whose sight repulsed us and our minds devoured
the spiciest foods that traced acidic burps after sahoor

let us give thanks this eid
to the erasing of raw aches of the body
the nightly chase of ellipsis to essence
the testing of boundaries of nerves and compassion

let us give thanks this eid
to the land of plenty where some perpetually fast

the mourners of the dead, those shot but not in the nation's memory
the bounty of mothers torn from wailing children,
we too create the disappeared

let us give thanks this eid
the pathological haters conserving a gold-plated past with treason
the craving, intolerant heart
the ever-blind, the ever-deaf, the ever-dumb
to this soil slaking blood, the trails of tears, the jingles of coins and chains,
the camps in the desert, the burning crosses, children in cages

let us give thanks this eid and remember

Autumn Lessons
by F. Marzia Esposito
translated by Jeanne Bonner

There's fog in the courtyard when I go out back. It's appeared now for three days in Milan. It slows everything down, the fog. It immobilizes things. Even the black row of garbage cans behind the restaurant seems to take on a certain attitude; they have a greater sense of composure.

I look up at the buildings forming the four sides of the courtyard around me. The laundry hangs out to dry, so many colorful squares of cloth in the faded air. And the landings in front of the tenements that line the courtyard, their doors facing outward. So beautiful, I think. Pami is emptying the compost bin. When she's finished, there's the sound of tin, the dull thud of the lid as it vibrates.

"Where is he?" I ask.

"I suggest you keep your distance. He's really pissed off right now. It was a mad house here last night. He had to take over serving for you and people were grumbling because the food was taking forever to come."

"It was an emergency."

"He doesn't give a shit."

"I'll explain it. Just where is he?"

I close the door gently after her. As soon as I step inside, I see Ros standing in the middle of the dining room, with his legs spread wide, staring at me. I only manage to open my mouth before he says, "You're fired."

I don't even put up a fight. I line up my heels, my bag pressed tightly to my side, and I'm gone. What's always screwed me when it comes to men is my insistence that I can get by one way or another without their help. In any event, I have the day off, 600 euros to make it through the month, my resume to copy and the wheel turning again. The city widens before me with each step; I move forward and the city becomes immense. The traffic means nothing to me; I don't need to rush, I'm not cold and I don't even have the strength to despair. Along the street there are lots of moving shadows and the trees look as though they are lit on fire by the sun. I have a city at my disposal, but I have no intention of taking advantage of it.

I open the door to my building, take my mail from the mailbox and enter my apartment. Intesa Bank has written to me and there's a notice from a certain Mr. Gas Company.

The silence of the empty rooms kills me. I turn on the TV, undress and sit in front of the screen in a t-shirt and my underwear. They're showing a live image of people in boats and the TV announcers are saying these people want to come to Italy, that in Italy everything is better, there's work. I'm in the mood for something crunchy. I use one hand to open a packet of crackers, chewing them while I turn on the shower with my other hand. I have all Saturday and half of Sunday free; this is Max's weekend. I can't even start looking for work. I think I will just take a lot of showers. A lot of showers.

The sensation of my skin being sponged over by the hot steam soothes me. My face has been erased, I feel as though it's featureless, a fleshy mask without openings. No one can see me anyway. I pad over the tiles, leaving watery footprints with my dripping wet heels, then I stop to pick up from the hallway floor the little blue truck with flames on the sides. I put it on Lori's desk. His silver cape is balled up on his bed. I fold it in half, then in half again. Lori's things are waiting for him. Just like me, come to think of it. My bathrobe vibrates. I see a telephone number on my cell that I don't know.

I pick up. "*Pronto*?"

"How are you?"

Nice work, I think, never saving anyone's name in the phone.

"Fine," I say.

"Well, I'm fine, too," he says.

I have a vague recollection of this guy—he's hot, a friend of Pami's, and a complete stranger. I say nothing and wait.

"I've heard you're not working tonight—"

"Well, that's a euphemistic way of putting it."

He goes on. "—and since you're not working, I was thinking we could grab a beer together."

"We can celebrate me getting fired."

I can feel him smile down the phone line. *You want to sleep with me? Find someone else*, I think.

My towel keeps getting colder so I go in my room. There I undo the towel wrapped around my head like a turban and I rub my hair dry with my left hand. In the other hand, I hold the phone.

"I would but I've already made plans. I'm going to see a movie."

"Oh really. Which one?"

Right—which one? "*Il posto delle fragole*," I say.

"Did that just come out?"

Oh sure. It's brand new, I think to myself. Or it was in 1957. The useless things you learn when you graduate with a degree in Film Studies. There's a moment of silence on the line, but without any tension. At least not for me. As far as I am concerned, we could sit here in silence forever.

"Well, I guess we'll just try another time."

"Yep, another time," I say, echoing his words.

When I hang up, my feet are freezing, I absolutely have to put on a pair of socks. In the strip of a mirror hanging on the wall, my nude body is cut off. But if I stand in profile, I can see my whole body. I do that and

I see my shoulder blades jutting out, too bony, my back and my round, adolescent breasts. In a few years, I won't still look like this, so I should take advantage while I am still young. I really should force myself to do what all the other women do—imitate them, copy their moves. Actions convey thoughts. That way I would learn the right intentions—I'd move on, without indulging my innate tendency to avoid. That's how I prefer it.

I don't know how to act in certain situations. Or maybe I don't want to know how. I'm like a piece of frozen meat that's been left in the middle of a glacier. It doesn't break free and become unstuck—it thickens. Giving the block of meat a kick isn't a solution. You move it from A to B but you don't change its nature.

I turn on my other side. If I suck in my stomach, each individual rib sticks out enough that you can count them. I'm a freakin' little girl. Yep—*I look like a girl*, I think. I look like a girl—which means I am not one anymore.

While I grab a pair of panties and a t-shirt from my bureau, a message comes in: "Mommy I make you a pikture." In life, we're each given one good thing. And mine is Lori.

I eat, I have something to drink and I watch TV and more TV and more TV and...When I open my eyes next, I feel pins and needles in my shoulder. My arm is rigid; it just hangs there, numb, as if I'd been shot up with Novocain. I search for the remote control under the couch cushions with my good arm and I turn off the TV. The murmur of voices disappears and visually, I'm plunged once again into a world of static.

I look at my phone and I see the tiny, bright green envelope icon is flashing. I have two messages: "How was the film……?" The ellipsis seems to never end. Maybe if I took all the dot-dot-dots and put them together, I'd get the drawing of the guy fishing who catches an old shoe? Do I delete the message or reply? I open the other message: "Mommy I brushed my tooths. I'll bring you chestnuts tomorrow. *Buonanotte.*"

I mitigate the silence in the house by cleaning. The detergent burns my eyes and makes my nostrils flare. Cleaning is therapeutic for me. I feel useful. It gives me a precise focus and a task I can complete. At first, everything is dirty. Then it's clean. Action, then result. Sensible, necessary activities.

I get hungry at 3 o'clock. Twenty minutes later, I'm already snoozing. I dream I'm in some speed warp dimension and I'm falling through the air. And while I'm falling – right before the impact – I hear the doorbell ring. The sound separates from my nose dive fall and I'm momentarily split in two.

I come to from my sleep, annoyed; it was such a pleasant fall. I open my eyes and go to answer the buzzer.

"It's me," she says.

If there's one thing I hate, it's people who show up unannounced. I press the button to let her in then I hear the sound of the large front door of my apartment building clicking open.

"Did something happen?" I ask.

She comes inside and I close the door securely. She moves through the apartment with a blast of caramel scent trailing behind her. She uses those creams that smell like refined sugar. Looking around, her eyes swoop over the walls again and again.

"Wow, this house is as clean as a whistle."

"Every other Sunday," I say.

I start to make coffee while she remains standing. She's wearing killer heels and is dressed as though she is headed out for a night *in discoteca.* She pulls a chair out from the table so she can hang her jacket.

"So he's already replaced me," I reply after she fills me in on everything.

She gets up from the table and places her used coffee cup in the sink, then she leans her lower back against the edge of the table. I automatically scoot backwards to do the same. Her pelvis is right in front of me, as if it were staring at me. Her arms, though, are perched slightly above it, folded.

She nods in the direction of Lori's door. "And my little boyfriend? Where is he?"

"He's in the woods, gathering chestnuts with his father." *I used to like those woods, too,* I think.

"Good, we can get right to the heart of the matter."

I say nothing.

"Listen, my friend is good-looking and he does well for himself."

"Good for him."

"And he tells me he likes you. You have a certain way about you."

"What way?"

"A kind of weirdness."

"I'm not weird. Do you think I'm weird?"

"What does it matter what I think?"

"I mean, if I were weird, would you tell me?"

"Well, I'm not a guy."

"So I appear weird only to guys? I feel like I'm talking to my son. Boys, girls—as if there were real gender identities."

"If you say one more thing like 'gender identity,' I'm out of here."

I look over at the window. The weather is non-weather. What season is it? I don't know. They put up a sheet of plywood behind the glass. A piece of plywood where the horizon should be. I bump into it all the time, hitting my head because I am so insanely tired. Other people avoid it, they ignore it, as if it didn't exist.

"*Insomma*, how old are you?

"Can I ask what you want from me this morning, Pami?"

"It's not morning. Do you see what I mean? Don't you see what's happening to you?"

"OK, read my lips. I. Don't. Have. A. Job."

"You. Don't. Have. A. Man."

Great, let's get to the bottom of everything right now.

I go over to the bathroom to close the door. Lori's shoes are in the washer; as they move around inside, they bang rhythmically, creating a steady background noise, a percussion of soles. The same note. Always the same. I'm 33, I think. *Maledizione*. I'm 33 years old and in a flash, I'll be 40.

Eventually Pami says she has to go—something about a message she got. She collects her things in a hurry and is gone. It gets dark and I turn on all of the lights in the apartment so I don't have to see the spooky shadows on the walls when I walk around.

*

Lori runs past me in the hallway. He says he has to use the bathroom. I follow him with my gaze then I look back at Max's pained face. I keep my hand on the door knob. He's not coming in anyway. He readjusts his eyeglasses on the bridge of his nose; it's a new tic of his. He's been doing it over and over now for a few months. When we were together, he didn't do it, this tiny repetitive movement. It could drive you nuts.

But maybe he just needs to tighten the screws on the frames.

"How did it go?" I ask.

"*Bene.*"

"Is there something I need to know?" Is it about Sandra, I wonder? But I don't say it.

"No," he says. "Everything is okay. I'm just tired. We'll talk another time."

Once upon a time, I think, as I close the door. But it didn't go that way.

I look at my wrists, where the straps of the plastic bag full of chestnuts are cutting off blood to my hand. Not sure what I am going to do with them.

Lori's heavy stomping around the house revives me; I'm whole again, I think to myself. I order pizzas, then cut Lori's into pieces. He grabs slice after slice, completely concentrated on eating. As he's nibbling on a piece of crust, he informs me quite casually that he hasn't done his homework.

"Why didn't you do it on Saturday?"

"Do you know I beat him twice?" he asks triumphantly. "Twice!"

"All you did was play video games?"

"The Wii isn't a game."

He's 37, Max. Thirty-seven years old.

"Get the assignment," I say to Lori.

"I know what I have to do."

"Get the assignment."

He gets down from the chair and walks down the hall, dragging himself with a sulky air. A moment later he's back and he sits down. I move the plates, flip through the assignment quickly and then I look up. He's spread out under the table like a dead man, bits of his half-eaten dinner around him.

I point my finger squarely at his nose and he goes cross-eyed looking at it. His eyes distort as he stares.

"Listen and listen up good," I say. "I'm only going to do this because it's late. But it's the last time. Promise me that it's the last time."

"*Va bene*, I promise."

"Don't forget that you've promised."

"Yup."

"A promise is serious business."

"I know."

I quickly read the exercise we have to do. "You do two, and I'll do three."

"But you said you were going to do it!"

"You do two, I'll do three. Got it?"

He nods, and I have him pass me his pencil case. As I unzip it, each tooth in the zipper makes the "zzz" sound. I look for a pen.

"Mommy?"

"What is it?"

"What if Sandra and Max get married?"

I balance the pen on my middle finger while Lori props himself up by his elbow, his cheek resting in the palm of his hand. That man is becoming more and more of a stranger to me every day. We were always against marriage; it was the cornerstone of our relationship. It's my fault. I struggle to imagine a life that's anything other than predictable. I want nothing more than an average existence. A neutral spot without peaks and valleys, without any new development to deal with. I'm not even asking to be happy or whatever—I just want a long enough period of time without any changes.

Marriage. Fantastic. Just what we needed.

"Mommy?"

"That's their business," I tell him.

I look at the previous page to get back to what we're doing.

Right: three sentences about autumn.

My Big Gay Essay

Carley Moore

1.

When I was sixteen, my best friend and I found a bolt of bright, mustard yellow, polyester fabric in the clearance bin at Joanne Fabrics. We wanted to make wide-legged high-waisted pants—like I now see when I scan the racks at Top Shop—and long hip-hugging skirts. Neither of us had mastered zippers, but we were fine with an elasticized waistband. But it was the color that really got us. Nobody in our dying Rust Belt town wore this color. It was obnoxious and loud, not to be missed against the gray, dirt snow. We bought the whole bolt for maybe five bucks.

The fabric was so thick it jammed our sewing machines, but we re-threaded the needles and made two hideous pairs of big-legged pants. The waistbands were bunchy and uncomfortable because the elastic was big and also from the clearance bin. No matter. We loved them and wore them to school. Our few punk friends marveled at our DIY skills, while we withstood the usual attacks from football players and cheerleaders. Whispers and looks. Not like the beatings our male friends endured. The pants were uncomfortably hot because they were made of tires and plastics or whatever stew of pesticides and polymers made up

80s polyesters. If there were a fire, we'd have been burned alive by our pants. One of us may have gotten a yeast infection from wearing them. We were living a fantasy version of ourselves. We needed to believe we could make something out of nothing. That the ugly could become noteworthy and that we could turn garbage into couture. We didn't follow style rules. We made our own. We wanted to feel yellow—bright, futuristic, loud, while our town regularly told us that we were dirt.

One of the many brilliant threads in Andrea Lawlor's new novel, *Paul Takes the Form of a Mortal Girl*, is around the rituals of clothing—their power, their possibility for subversion, their ability to transform us, and the way they situate and complicate our genders. Paul, who has a kind of superpower, and can transform his body into a woman's body (with a spongy vagina) and sometimes a more masculine male body (with a bigger penis), has a talent for clothing and fantasy among other less bankable skills. In the middle of the novel, Paul moves to San Francisco to recover from a break-up in Provincetown, where he lived as Polly for several months. The narrator admits:

> Paul had to have a job. But maybe not drag. He walked and listed his other known talents: pouring beer without too much head, shoplifting, washing dishes, organizing items, knowing what was going to fashionable a little bit early, thrifting, clever commentary, introducing people to other people, cutting pictures out of magazines with x-acto knives, knowing when people where open to having sex, having sex, being gay. (227)

I still count some of these things as my talents, and still one has to have a job. Sigh. I don't want to give too much of the novel away, but Lawlor is so deft at recreating that early nineties, Generation X, slacker, queer, state school milieu, that I fell nostalgically back into the time where

I spent hours pulling together an outfit for a party, took the campus bus everywhere, and held several different jobs while trying to cobble together my $150 a month rent. And yet the novel is futuristic and almost sci-fi in its ideas about gender—as mutable, as ever changing, and a physicality we can mostly control at will with our minds.

2.

My dad's favorite movie is *Blade Runner*. I like to joke with my therapist that I'm a replicant, your basic pleasure model. I find this comforting, and my neurological disorder often leaves me with joint pain that makes me feel robotic and spastic. My father raised my brother and I to believe we were part of a special tribe, that there is nobody else like us. Misunderstood smarties. Robots. Replicants. Aliens to our own planet.

To be raised by a narcissist father is to learn quickly how to mirror and please. My father has always liked me best when I am staring into his face, nodding along with his story, and not saying a word. Growing up, he liked to play full albums for my brother and I while we sat trapped on the couch. Sometimes they were amazing—my father introduced me to Prince, R.E.M., Steely Dan, The Pretenders, The Talking Heads, and Z.Z. Top. There was also Molly Hatchett, AC/DC, and Metallica. Once, while a born-again Christian family improbably ate dinner at our atheist table, my father insisted on playing "Darling Nicki."

The mother of that family, whose daughter had shunned me at a Christian sleepaway camp I attended in a lame middle-school attempt to try new things, turned to me, with a sweetly evil smile and said, "Do you like this song?"

"I love Prince,"I might have said while my mother yelled, "They hate it. Turn it off!"

We were having one of our torture dinners. No matter the guests or if it was just us, we couldn't get along. My father, genuinely believed he could convert these bland white Christians into liking Prince. He thought if they could just listen, really listen, they'd get it. It was always like that with him. Pay attention. Stick with me. It will all make sense.

When my ex-husband and I separated, my father lamented, "But how will I see him?" A couple weeks later he accused me of "being gay and ruining my marriage." A couple months later, I decided to stop talking to him.

Oh shut up Dad, I wanted to say to him, *There are so many ways to ruin a marriage.*

3.

Earlier in *Paul Takes the Form of a Mortal Girl*, Paul as Polly sits in a cafe with their girlfriend Diane in Provincetown. Diane wants to help set free an abused dog and is annoyed with Polly for lacking focus:

> Paul looked down at his burgundy cords, his black Runways tee shirt (a church thrift shop score in Orleans—how jealous would Jane be) tight over his waffled long-john shirt, his Save the Whales! belt buckle with its fresco humpback. He liked this new look, enjoyed this foray

> into androgynous style, liked the little fuck-you shadows of femininity he deployed. He wasn't trying to copy Diane, but he did like them to be complementary. He did manage to find a copy of *Times Square* at City Video and rented it for them to watch together, had tried to explain to her his thoughts on runaway tomboy rocker dyke gender, but she'd been unimpressed. Diane didn't like to talk about gayness very often. Paul estimated that he held back two out of five gay-themed comments. (201)

Androgynous style. The little fuck you shadows of femininity. Deployment and subterfuge. Hiding in plain sight. I've long used clothing to confuse myself, to confuse others, to register as unreadable or misplaced. I've been happiest at 21 and now in my mid-forties with short boyish hair. Baggy boyish clothes delight me, but I'm often in dresses that are technically inappropriate for the occasion. I sometimes teach in a silver sequined dress because it cheers me up. I wear yoga pants everywhere. I use a jean jacket as a suit coat. I wear bikinis to show my stretch marks. I hate seeing fellow moms in beach dresses, though I totally get the desire to cover up. The truth is, I don't often see myself. Can we ever really see ourselves from the outside? Our asses especially? The backs of our necks? There is the image we think we give off and something far more complicated that gets transmitted to the world.

There was that leather/pleather leaf print tie-dyed jacket I bought in Albany with Janna. A neon green and black mini-skirt from Betsy Johnson, a $15 Century 21 score. A mint green lozenge of a dress, stitched on a machine like my mother used to make us matching yellow lace wedding dresses. Those purple and black combat boots, faux Fluevog. I wore those to book Writing Center appointments, meet drunks at Sophie's and Mars Bars, and to lie across laps in the backseats of cabs. The TJ Max bras I buy with Stef and the drawstring skirt my daughter and I stitched for Genevieve the rabbit.

When I used the gender conversion app on Facebook, the only thing it adds is stubble. I feel this is another hint for me, that I'm circling something I need to figure out.

"But you only write about your relationships with men," my friend is pushing me at a bar. She's femme, identifies as a lesbian, and is a truth teller. I take it in because listening is something I can do.

"That's true," I admit. "This is new to me. I haven't been in a relationship with a woman. I make out with them, I'm attracted to them, but I want to do more, and I need to write about it."

There is more to this conversation. Another good friend is there too. We are talking about openness, tenderness, risks, and dogs.

We are talking about a woman I met two weeks ago at a poetry reading. We wandered around together with a small crowd afterwards. She stayed close to me, said things like, *You know where to go.*

Everyone left. We had the dim divey back room of the bar to ourselves. We were magnetized. Mouths. Lips. Hands. I slid my hands under her shirt, rubbed at her jeans. She put her hands down my pants. I was wearing period underwear, which is like a chastity belt. I felt an ideological wall falling down. I am a Gemini and we can be sloppy with our love. I had some tequila. What is gender? What is a dick or a man anyway? My whole life I've been taking care of dicks, petting, sucking, rubbing them and maybe I don't have to all of the time? Maybe it's not about gender at all, but people, a person. I sound like I haven't read any theory on anything, but I've read it all. I should quote Butler,

Sedgewick, Preciado, or Halberstam, but I'm not feeling it. I've got Lawlor. They are my theory. The novel is theory at its most embodied form I think. I'm not a person who "hates labels," and I'm not trying to be dodgy. I'm confused sometimes. I hate binaries. I am often two or three things at once. I'm queer. Bisexual. There I wrote it. If anything I think too much, and suffer from deep earnestness.

We stumbled out of that bar. We ate pizza and stared out the window at the stupid, gentrifying East Village. We kept touching each other. We talked about another woman we both have a crush on, a mutual friend who confused us. I told her about my boyfriend. She told me about her wife. We love them both very much. We talked about our rules for openness. We didn't improbably go home together.

4.

There's something very silly about coming out at 45. I mean, like, who cares? I find myself back in my state school town, like Paul in Lawlor's novel, feeling nostalgic for all my gay best boyfriends and their coming out to me. My response was often, "I know and it's great and I love you." But I shouldn't have said "I know," because it takes away the drama of it, the declaration, the announcement that felt so important in the 90s and maybe still does.

I tell my mother on the phone and she says, "I'm not surprised."

"How come?" I ask.

"Because you like to go to Long Island with S and D," as if traveling with a queer couple means anything in particular.

"And you can't live here." She's referring to the dying gray dirt town I left but where everyone in my family still lives. My dear mom, who is always looking for reasons to explain why I left her, why I had to move away to the big city and live such a precarious life.

"But mom," I tease, "That's not why I can't live there. I mean I feel like a big dyke when I'm home. I don't look like anyone else, they stare. It's bad there. There are no jobs there for me, no thing I can do. It's so small, I'd suffocate."

"Everybody stares here," she's been saying this to me my whole life. In my teens and twenties, it drove me crazy. It felt like an excuse, a cop out. But now I find it cute. My mom is 70. Like most of the women in her family, she is improbably healthy. Tough. Fit. Totally with it mentally.

I don't want anything to happen to her. I want us to know each other as fully as possible. We've come a long way in our relationship.

"It's okay," she says.

"I know."

And then she starts telling me about the weather and a book she's reading.

5.

During the first year of my marriage to a man, who is now my ex-husband, dear friend and the father of my child, I wandered around the yellowed, gilded streets of Florence. I was lucky to be there! I was teaching in Tuscany! Everyone told me so! But I was profoundly lonely. I didn't speak Italian. I had no interest in the Renaissance, though I would learn to love David's muscled ass and Fra Angelico's dreamy frescos in their cold monk's cells. I liked to visit Fra Savonarola's hair shirt—a slab of soft leather affixed with porcupine quills. I visited it often to stare at its painful beauty. It wasn't anything like a shirt. More like a belt or a brace. I used to wear leg braces. I hated them, but this was an object of choice. I never consented to those braces which later deformed my feet. I could choose to wear a hair shirt. There was also a self-flagellation stick. A small wooden rod with a tiny whip affixed to the end of it. I coveted that hair shirt because I wanted to feel something instead of sadness. I wanted it to hurt me in the ways I have since wanted my doms to hurt me. I wanted to be under its control so I wouldn't have to think or do anything.

What hurt me most in Florence was that I had no friends. I had gone from a huge circle of loving friends to knowing no one except my husband. He was good company, but he wasn't enough. I had never learned how to be alone. Now I know but it took a divorce and a lot of therapy to just appreciate solitude and not panic. Eventually, I made a friend. An American who had fallen in love with an older Italian man. I would have been miserable without her.

Later, when I came back to Brooklyn, I still had that same feeling. An emptiness. A longing for something I couldn't name. I thought I wanted a baby. I did. Eventually, after a whole bunch of medicine and loss, I had her. She changed my life, made me want to get better, and there is no one I love more in this world, but she didn't fill that hole. No person can fill the kind of hole I'm writing about here.

I still wandered around Brooklyn feeling lost. Waiting for something to happen. The wind on street corners whipping through my then mom bob. The stroller catching on the lip of the curb. The feeling that I was always playing a part very badly, especially at certain playdates with very straight moms who lived in beautiful apartments I would never be able to afford. I didn't want to talk about nursing or baby clothes or my husband's accomplishments. I wanted to talk about bad thoughts and books that did not sell a lot of copies and sex or not sex. I found some moms like me. It took a while. Most of them were poets.

6.

A vagina is a hole to put things into. A pussy is a hole. Hole is a band I still love. There is a book by Maurice Sendak that my kid and I loved called *A Hole is To Dig*. This is the part of the essay where I would like to riff and free associate. It's a place for you to get lost with me the writer. It's a tidal pool or a portal. Maybe it's just distraction or play. The poet in me. Puns. Do you remember a store on lower Broadway called Wholesale Liquidators? They had everything. Forks. Clock radios. Shoes. Now we are stuck with Whole Foods, when really everything we do is piece work. I don't know how to make the parts into a whole. Holy moly. I miss the voice I used to read to my kid when she was really little. It was like many puppet voices. I mostly only use it on cats now. Pussies. Isn't that what sent Earnest Hemingway screaming away from Paris? Gertrude calling to Alice, "Here pussy, pussy, pussy?"

I have wanted more than anything in my life to be my whole self, however complicated and messy that may seem to my family or my partners, but mostly I have not been able to locate my selves or I have hidden them so deep that when they emerge I'm surprised.

I met her six weeks ago. Since I started working on this essay, my boyfriend has left me or maybe I made it so unbearable for him that he had to go. Maybe we are taking a break. Maybe we are okay. Maybe I forgot that I wanted to be free and I lost my way. Maybe I like exploding safe things in Rom Com high drama style. In my experiences with them, cis gendered straight men do a lot of crazy shit. They stop talking. They lie. They threaten to kill themselves. They disappear. They ghost. They pretend everything is okay. They gaslight. Maybe women do all of that too.

I never wrote about him because I sensed he did not want me to.

I texted my brother and mother about my boyfriend leaving and my brother, ever my loving foil, texted, "You can't have two guys, two girls, or a guy and a girl. All illegal moves. Good try though. Flew too close to the sun." I lol.

I sent them a Selena Gomez shrug/smile meme and then we started to text about the kids.

I like that I am the Icarus of my family, the weirdo artist with some crazy escape plan, but I'm not trying to die. Still, I am grateful to their love and humor around my coming out. It has given me strength.

A few weeks earlier I came out to my brother in a text. He texted back, "No worries, Nibbs (his nickname for me since we were kids). I kind of knew a little. I love you always."

I am a quick study. I learn to use my mouth. There is a magical toy. Later it's mostly my hand. The next day my arm quivers and my thighs are weak from exertion. One time when she comes, she punches herself by accident and sees stars. I open and close my thighs. Again and again and again. *Our bodies fit together perfectly*, I think, *because there is no dick in the way.*

Meanwhile I am reading some books. One is the self-help classic *Co-Dependent No More* by Melanie Beatty and the other is Michelle Tea's amazing new collection of essays, *Against Memoir*. In one of my favorite essays is, "On *Chelsea Girls*" which is love letter to Eileen Myles and their determination to tell their own lesbian, working class story, "just my part" (56). Tea writes about reading *Chelsea Girls* and lesbian sex and her own young curiosity about it:

> However, the secret is, everyone, especially perhaps lesbians, must learn to have sex, must teach themselves and one another, constantly charging up against the limitations of assumption and convention and imagination, not to mention the body. (51)

And later:

> Queer sex could feel like children's make believe and a carnival haunted house and a lion devouring an antelope. It could feel like psychic surgery and a new-fangled workout routine and an aggressive cuddle fest. (52)

I was underlining the book furiously as I read, partly because I was lucky enough to get to interview Tea, so I wanted to take good notes, but I was also reading this book, the way I read many favorite writers, as spirit guides, as self-help, and because I desperately needed some instructions.

I did have to learn to have sex with her. We had to teach each other, I had to imagine a new world for myself, and it was like everything Tea described, and more because each body has its own landscapes, smells, wounds, birthmarks, and pleasures regardless of gender. And to calm me down, she kept whispering, “Don’t worry. We’re just bodies.”

7.

I missed him and I cried all night. We spoke on the phone. I was afraid and then I fell asleep. I woke up and watched Janelle Monae’s “Emotion Picture,” (*Dirty Computer*) and cried some more. Recognition. Love. Pleasure. The white police state with its whirring insect-like police bugs. The white state in which I reap enormous benefit and am mostly safe, except for when I stand up with my feminist sisters of color and get yelled at or sued or told to shut up, mostly by other white people. But I am never arrested. I am never chased. I am never harassed by the whirring drones. I am never shot.

I am so grateful to Monae for coming out, though she is eclipsing my coming out in every way. Lol. Bisexual. Queer. Pansexual. I am so grateful for this new language from radicals who are younger than me. It’s more complicated. I need it.

I think of some of my favorite lines from Gloria Anzaldua’s, groundbreaking essay “La Conciencia de la Mestiza: Toward a New Consciousness” which I first read as an undergraduate. It spoke to the mix (Swedish, Cuban, German, English, French) in me and still does though I recognize it as utopian. Though aren’t all consciousness changing texts? Anzaldua argues, “As a mestiza I have no country, my homeland cast me out; yet all countries are mine because I am every woman's sister or potential lover" (389). I want this to be true. She wrote it in 1987, but for me I know it would be a reach, a grab I can't make. Still, utopias. Sigh.

I see a bit of this mestiza consciousness in *Dirty Computer*. In much of the movie, Monae's character has a boyfriend and a girlfriend. She crosses several landscapes simultaneously and claims futuristic countries as her own.

And some lyrics just stick in my head, like the dirty computer I am. Like the robot, replicant, I was raised and not raised to be.

> *Pink, like the secrets you hide.*
> *I want a crazy, classic life.*
> *Your code is programmed not to love me.*

8.

The day before, I dropped my kid off at school and walked under a crane. It was blocking the street and about to heft something out of a gutted soon-to-be-renovated billion-dollar townhouse. I stopped to watch. I hate cranes—for a couple of years in NYC, they kept falling on people—but I was curious. What was this house's secret? What would I get to see? A man joined me. He was dressed nicely, but barefoot. He had the look of someone on edge, manic. Going shoeless in New York is a particular choice. Still, he stood next to me, calm. We waited. The crane slowly pulled its long arm out of the shell of the house to reveal. Wait. For. It. A tangle of wires and cords. The electric lint ball of the house maybe. A tumbleweed of nothing. I sighed and walked away. I'd wanted treasure—an old piano, a faded rose-colored couch from the 1920s, a claw-foot tub. I wanted the crane to unearth a secret. But there wasn't one.

"What is the Difference between Globalization and Neoliberalism?"

Amy Sara Carroll

Last week someone asked me, "What is the difference between globalization and neoliberalism?" The question isn't as innocent as it sounds. If all of us are imprecated in the cat-and-mouse game of cause and effect, who wouldn't apprehend the pair—at the bare minimum—as kissing cousins to the twin towers? Sure to go down, in historical terms, this is how the world turns: purgative reportage from Iraq serves as the perennial reality-check, presumptive as the corrective, Well, at least, I don't live in Fallujah. Packing a one-two punch, purple-hearted Michigan slumps deeper into the driver's seat of depression. Aggressively passive, voters pass Proposition 2, designer-drug legislation with the intent to euthanize affirmative action (euphemised "The Civil Rights Initiative"), even as the state's Supreme Court rescinds queer Michiganders' bare-boned benefits. I wonder, Where did I move? A friend explains to me the intricacies of false advertising, Here is the shape of the mitt, we're somewhere to the thumb's Left. Directionally impaired, tone-deaf, I take cartography in like a fist. Stone-butch blues infuse the landscape with touching resistance. Industry, like a snow-bird, flexes its mobile muscles, while, individuals (hermetically sealed) orchestrate equally market-driven Jackie Brown heists of citizenship. I will grant you the once removed diehard few who stay put for museums' erections. One for the auto, two for the Arab-American, three for the Motor City's revitalization (Don't mourn, organize). In the hospital,

I sit elongated hours with my son. A woman eyes us and no one in particular, Is your kid Mexican? Calloused malice, like a flag at half-mast, hangs haggard as her expression when summoned. Six degrees of separation, peripheral as vision, somebody's piling it on: Once upon a time, it would have made a world of difference to partake of the blue pill instead of the red. Let's split the difference—civilization and its discontents, globalization/neoliberalism, the New World's Borderization. How schmaltzy to recycle the local's ashes when the trans-planted's rejection looms, imminent as an organ. The chickens have come home to roost, environmentalism's ogres are loose, and we can only talk about the whether. Or not. Underground, centrifugal truth pacts a Faustian plot. Lot's pillar salts and melts, but recasts its lot with the dammed—"new ethnicities" on the horizon that slouch toward Bethlehem, terra-forming interactive screens. The night is young, middle age, a means to an end. Sipping creature comforts, pretend that the performatively tautological amends the conciliatory constellations of History, that the sciences of fiction stand on the shoulders of their own—two feet under. If you follow this totemically taboo logic, even planets become subaltern subjects. Witness Pluto's recent downgrade. Now try to make an alternate case for the "Recline of the West." Expect nothing less than a free Fall into the postscriptual.

Oops!

Rosamond S. King

Careful we have to be

: Opening the door

, Getting our wallets

, Playing in a park

, Switching lanes

Can be fatal

.Ask? There is no ask

.Try? There is no try

.There is only shoot

.Accidental slaughter

Is an epidemic

In the abattoir

And on the rez

REPARATIONS

Rosamond S. King

see   through   people!

on sale today!

35 year old   boys   and girls

breeding boys

    to lighten your race

breeding girls

    for fun and profit

backs bent every morning

legs open every night

see   through   people!

cheap!

Firelei Báez on Generosity and Freedom in Art

Angie Cruz

I met Firelei Báez at The Andy Warhol Museum for over an hour. She was taking a short break from installing her one-woman show *Firelei Báez: Bloodlines*. That day, high school students had been recruited to help her paint the walls, built especially for the show. Jessica Beck, the curator, had been painting alongside Firelei. The spirit and energy around the show reminded me of my Dominican family back home, when something had to get done, everyone rolled their sleeves and just got to work. The following is our conversation.

Angie Cruz: I'm thrilled that you currently have a solo show at The Warhol. I have been thinking a lot about the invisibility of Latino/a artists in mainstream media and and it's exciting for Pittsburgh, and for me personally, as a Dominicana, to have you here. In an interview you said that you've had the experience of being the first Latina/o or Caribbean artist to present in a museum. Why do you think that is, in 2017?

Firelei Báez: Latino and Caribbean artists have been working within mainstream American institutions all through history. Take Gordon Matta Clark for instance, who was of Chilean descent but is solely cited as an American Artist. It is through the efforts of courageous academics and artists within the last thirty or so years that artist like myself can

Firelei Báez: Bloodlines Installation, The Andy Warhol Museum, photo Abby Warhola

proudly claim our Caribbean seat at the table. I am the first Caribbeña artist to have a solo show at The Warhol Museum.

AC: You once said that if you went way back, you'd cite Leonardo da Vinci as an influence. But then more contemporarily, you cited Felix Gonzalez-Torres and Ana Mendieta as influences.

FB: We have such a broad lexicon to look onto. Da Vinci's book of drawings was the first art book I ever saw and that was in my sophomore year of high school. I really love Julie Mehretu's work, and although there are some amazing male artists, I've been trying to make an effort to put focus on at least three women artists who are canonical and who have shifted my idea of art. For me they are Lorna Simpson and Julie Mehretu. I love love the work of Kara Walker, Wangechi Mutu and Simone Leigh. Also writers like Arundhati Roy, Zadie Smith and Julia Alvarez—

AC: What's interesting about many of the artists you mentioned is that they identify as African-American artists. So for you as a Dominican—

FB: I think generally in the U.S. the younger generation of Dominican artists are more informed by African American art. Many of the Dominican artists in D.R. who were successful, moved to Paris, they looked to Europe and came from a certain class. So as a Dominican raised in the U.S. but who spent my formative years in the D. R., I didn't grow up with any concept of art. It was through public schooling and after school programs in the U.S. that I was like, oh art is something that people do. I made art all the time–my family is super creative and I would be the one to make paper dolls for the entire neighborhood–so the act of making was always with me, but this idea of becoming an artist, I didn't have that in D.R.

AC: This was also true for me as a writer. I was greatly informed by slave narratives, and writers like Baldwin and Morrison. When I read them I was like, this is my story too.

FB: Yeah it's the parallel. It's like our story is so complex that in choosing to tell it, you have to have a filter. Discourse in the U.S. is–black or white–there isn't the multivalence you'd have in Latin America. I think it comes in part out of religion. Catholicism allows for all these different threads, syncretism. You can't have images in Protestant religions for instance, so you need very clear ideas of what is and can't be. Have you seen casta paintings from Latin America?

AC: No, I haven't.

FB: They're these paintings that told their owners who they were to society based on their race mixture to the nth degree. They existed within the Catholic religion and were usually displayed near the home's altar, with the saints that were meant to be prayed to on a daily basis. In these spaces, people were encouraged to mix, with this goal of being mestizo—a very white blend though. In all of the casta paintings, at every level, you'll see someone mixing with black. They were supposed to enact a kind of social violence, but at the same time they are some of the first intimate, and very tender portraits of mixed families.

AC: I'm so happy you're saying this about Protestantism versus Catholic aesthetics, because when I teach books by people of color in particular, some students will say, it's interesting but I just don't feel it? And I understand how they feel because that's how I feel about certain writing in the U.S. that are often celebrated. For years I have been thinking about how our spiritual formation inform our aesthetic leaning and

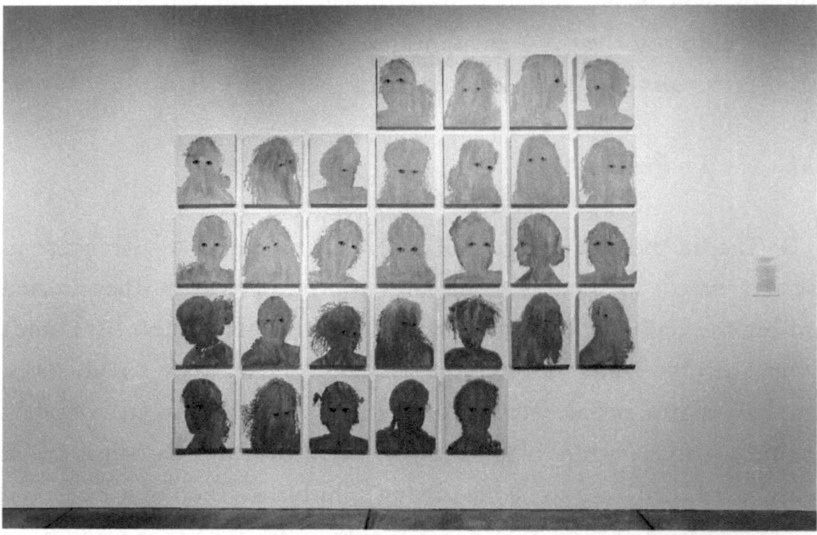

Firelei Báez, Can I Pass? Introducing the Paper Bag to Fan Test for the Month of June, 2011, courtesy the artist and Gallery Wendi Norris, San Francisco, image courtesy of Pérez Art Museum Miami, courtesy of Freese Family Collection.

consumption of culture. As a younger writer in the MFA workshop I was often told my work had too many characters, too much drama. But when I read certain works, I think, I need more drama. To me, when I see your visual work I understand a Dominicaness in it. There's this rich, multi-sensory provocation. I *feel* it.

FB: Thank you. They don't know how much restraint we have to put on ourselves to show only a fraction of our experiences. There is so much more to say and this is just the needle's eye being allowed at this moment. We as immigrants have access to all this information, all these rich complex histories which we have no problem understanding and translating because we're used to seeing ourselves as Other, and Other in ourselves.

AC: I feel like there's definitely a lot of momentum for African American art and literature right now in the U.S.. How do you feel about the reception for works from the Spanish-speaking Caribbean?

FB: It's funny, I'm a Dominican citizen, but I was raised here. My accent's American, my sense of the world is American, a lot of the work I've made wouldn't have been made if I'd been raised in the Dominican Republic. My work addresses race and class and in D.R. they would be like, what's wrong with your brain? Why are you speaking about these issues? Because they think that they don't exist or are addressed differently. I exist as a bridge. In this in-between space. Right now, I'm either Latin American or I'm American. The art collections are built around those two identity politics. So someone like me has to choose a camp. There's no space for that in-between.

AC: The borderland.

FB: Exactly. With the Latinx movement, it's the idea of valuing that space, of making it a valid voice with concrete weight. But right now I either have to be Latin American or Black. If I show too much at Studio Museum in Harlem then El Museo del Barrio resents it.

AC: Really?

FB: I've experienced that. They'll be like, oh she's all black now. Oh no, she's all Latina. You can't be enough of this or enough of that. The black diaspora is bigger than the United States. Take Brazil or even the island of Martinique. That tiny Caribbean island had more African slaves brought there than the entirety of the U.S. before the Louisiana Purchase. We in the African diaspora share a range of similar experiences, perhaps to a greater degree outside the United States. Conversations around race in the U.S. are so didactic, you're either one or the other. This in part drove, in my opinion, the clarity of the discourse and policies of the Civil Rights movement. In romance language-speaking spaces, like Brazil and Latin America, race is always addressed in terms of mestizaje, supposedly never prizing one race over the other, but in all honesty pushing for a more European ending.

AC: What about U.S. Latino/a art? Where does it fit?

FB: What's held as the canon of Latin American art is usually very European modernism. In every sphere, you're following this very specific European model, and usually the people who are showing in that are of a certain class. There's an artist now, Carmen Herrera for instance, she's a Cuban woman artist who got her first Whitney biennial at almost a hundred years old. Where is she being placed now? Think about the fact that she went to Paris in her twenties, and spent about eighty percent of her life in the U.S. Anyone reading through this would be like, she's

Firelei Báez: Bloodlines Installation, The Andy Warhol Museum, photo Abby Warhola

Latinx, she's a Latina, she's Cuban-born but spent most of her life here in the U.S.. She is being positioned within high modernism in Brazil. With artists like Lygia Clark and Hélio Oiticica. That's how they can find value in her work. There was latino/a work being done even before the WPA, and hopefully that work will be written about differently.

AC: In the book industry many people collapse latino/a and latin American books in the same lists. Often time the books are translations. In some ways it creates less visibility to the dearth of U.S. Latino/a narratives and still fuel the idea that we are foreigners. Don't you think?

FB: In a recent news cast there was a segment on immigration. During the caller segment a man asked "how are they vetting Puerto Ricans?" And the person taking the calls was like, you do realize they're American citizens? We don't prevent someone from Iowa coming to the main city, or someone from Hawai coming here. But this idea, because there's a different language being spoken perhaps, that you don't belong, or you're something that should be filtered out, is very heartbreaking.

AC: So you grew up in the Dajabon which is the border city between Dominican Republic and Haiti, loaded with a troubling history and also now very contentious. How has growing up in a space where there is a stark difference between the lush green environment of the Dominican Republic and then the deforested landscape of Haiti, has informed your work?

FB: Ok, so think of the French Enlightenment, the Empire, Parisian opulence: the money that fueled all of that was coming out of indigo and sugar from the colony of Saint- Domingue and Martinique. So that lush landscape we have in DR, that fertile soil, is all in Haiti as well. They were still paying billions of dollars in debt to France into the twentieth century for their independence. When Trujillo was doing the Massacre, they [Haiti] were still having to pay a huge embargo for their independence. I didn't even know this was possible until I was doing research on the palace of Sans Souci, near Cap Haitian. Dominican Republic paid a similar independence debt to Spain as well but slowly, while still being part of a global commerce. It's incredible that not only do you have this war, where you shed blood and tears, but then the legality of it is that to get back into world trade, you have to pay monetarily for your freedom.

AC: So we know all these things intellectually but I'm curious: one of your works that I find very provocative is the *Paper Bag Test*, for example. I love how the eyes come in–they cross the border of the Paper Bag Test. It's very haunting to look at the work.

FB: I wanted the viewer to come to terms with there being a human being behind all that.

AC: Skin comes up a lot in your work, projections of nature and the outside onto the skin. Why skin?

FB: So, it's not so much about skin itself but rather ideas around the body. Or ideas around what forms how we treat land and body. You can usually see this in how I position the figure in my work. Usually, if a figure is in a white ground, sort of just isolated on a picture, on a plane, it's referencing things like Carl Linnaeus's taxonomy. Which was first developed as a way for humans to 'factually' tally the living beings and plants around them; but instead allowed for horrible things to be done to people and nature outside of Europe. The Dutch believe there were cannibals and vampires along with beavers and moose in the new world for instance. It's more of the body as a specimen that can be explored in order to reveal something of the viewer in the process. Any of my Ciguapa paintings would be an example of this. They are usually very physical, heavy seeming figures that fuse with landscape.

If the figure has a ground, then it is more about creating this void or space that diffuses the weight of the body. The surrounding color voids all that physicality and gets closer to spirit for me, to a psychological interiority. These near abstractions act like Rorschach's where the viewer projects themselves onto the picture. It is perhaps more freeing and intimate for me in the studio.

AC: Historically, skin has always been like the container, the separation from the outside world, but now we understand that skin is the communicator, the interface. Even the way we think about skin has changed so much. Also, thinking about communicating the projection, not just of other people but of nature, and in some ways it gives agency to nature.

FB: I completely agree. Some experiences as a kid really gave me a concrete understanding of that. When I was a kid I was told to control how I shed my hair, and for me it seemed so strange because it's very much like European witchcraft or voodoo, melding of East and West. Every part of your physical self is tied to your spirit, or who you are. So one of the biggest warnings was that if my hair was taken by a bird, I'd be stuck in limbo, because they exist between heaven and earth. And that would be the worst scenario, because you would have no agency whatsoever. You'd lose control of your body.

AC: I love that.

FB: As a little girl, I was taught to be beholden to nature. To think of it as something with immense power that can control you. But coming to the States, the birds are grooming princesses on TV. These humans are masters of everything in their environment. Coming from the Dominican Republic I was like 'listen girl, you're in danger!, your body and your soul are tied together, and if anything takes it, your control is gone.

AC: So you were in Miami when you decided to go to Cooper Union. Your family was good with that decision?

FB: They never were. I think they're coming to terms with it now because I'm doing things.

AC: You're very successful!

FB: But even now they're just like, ok maybe. They're like: you need health insurance, you need to have a husband, this many kids, you need to have a home, you need to have this car, and then we'll see if you're successful.

AC: So what do you think about this precarious moment for artists. Trump threats to cut NEA funding but also we're in a hyper-professionalized moment where if you're not a professional you kind of die, you know? I also like something that Angela Davis said about how our imaginations have been privatized, right? And thinking about what does that do to art?

FB: Here's the thing though. As a child of an immigrant, I knew to juggle several balls at the same time. So I know if this doesn't work… when I was in college I had five jobs sometimes. I can do *anything*.

AC: But what do you think the role of artists and writers is right now?

FB: Well, because art is being hyper-professionalized, it can create a certain rigidity in how you respond. And, yes ok we deserve to have quality of life, and maybe that's the biggest push toward professionalizing. If you are working for someone you shouldn't do it for free. But at the same time, there's more people working for free for institutions. Or art is being used as a band-aid to help the things that social policy isn't actually working on.

AC: Over the years I have seen some of my favorite museums move toward edutainment. I worked as a teaching artists at museum for years. And it was a great gig but I also think why are artists dropping into schools for a day? Schools should be creating dynamic curriculum where art is an everyday thing.

FB: But also, often art programs, directed to black and brown kids are geared toward how to improve their health, how to keep them from doing any crimes, how to make them not get pregnant. It's like it's never about art for itself and expressing their creativity. Art can help you break out of that confine and think bigger than where you're coming from.

AC: So in this moment, you're not terribly terrified for yourself or the world?

FB: Oh I am. I'm like, oh my god we're in the beginning of a dark age. What are we gonna do? But because– when I was growing up we'd spend summers with my grandmother and aunt who were Seventh Day Adventists, and for them, at the turn of the 20th century they were like, the world is gonna end! They've all been on rapture-wait mode for the past hundred years. Any time now, any time now! So even at the beginning of 2000 I was like, well we got two years! Just get ready. And when the world didn't end in 2000 I breathed a little and then I was like ok there's a future, let me start doing things that can help. Even though I have not been religious since I was twelve, that is still the mindset: be ready.

AC: For you, what were some of the main challenges as an artist?

FB: The roughest parts are not knowing where your income is going to be. Having to move several times. I went to a different school every year since I was in the first grade. I've just been ready for whatever comes. Just not being afraid of hard work. Which is a mindset you have to get out of after a certain point. Cause if you're on survival mode…it's like Maslow's Hierarchy of Needs. Yes, working your heart out helps you survive to a certain point but in order to really thrive you have to move beyond that and get to this point of, alright, well I belong in this space.

AC: Do you remember that moment?

FB: I might be just starting now. To go beyond survival. What would I do if I had to go beyond survival? What would I start expecting? What should I start establishing? I don't think I'm there yet. I probably need five more years of continuous feedback to feel like, ok, what's next?

AC: This is always a difficult question for me but I'm going to ask it to you anyway. Who is your ideal audience? And who do you think you're seeking feedback from?

FB: Originally, and I've said this many times: I made work for my mom and my sisters. For people who share a similar history to mine. And if that history happens to strike a chord in someone who has a different experience, then that's great. I'm always a little shocked and really happy when I've shown work in like Utah and Nevada, and there's still a chord, excitement. Because the histories I'm introducing to them are not familiar to a lot of people and sometimes not even to Dominicans themselves. If you give enough of a roadmap then many people might be excited to go and read more on it. So a woman of color is usually in my ideal audience.

AC: But if I look at your work without knowing the history, I would actually think, I really love the way that body is moving, for example. Or I'll be curious about why there's something happening in a certain way. I wouldn't necessarily know the history. So how do you communicate, like in your mind when you're communicating do you think like, I'm communicating it through beauty? Linguistically I'm just interested in...

FB: Well there's a visual seduction that happens, and then the sting, if you are actually generous enough to keep looking. I'm asking a lot of the viewer. And usually I want them to make it as much as I am. To meet me at a halfway point. I'll give enough for you to start creating the narrative. And a lot of people come in with their own histories. Especially if you're coming from another country. Folklore is a place that has so much overlap globally because we go through similar things no matter where you're coming from. So even when I'm talking about a Ciguapa from Hispaniola, there's a trickster figure that's extremely similar to it in Brazil, India or Ghana.

AC: I have two more questions. My first question is, if you had the ear of Trump for like two minutes and you asked him to look at three works—

FB: I don't think that's going to help. I would do this: I would take a course in hypnotism, I would go deep in that, and for those two minutes I would try to hypnotize him, the visuals could be anything, a Rauschenberg for instance.

AC: Are there any things that you think would help him see?

FB: I think the only thing that would help him to see would be to have his body be our body. The reason he doesn't see is because he doesn't need to see. His body, his children, the things he cares about are protected within his actions. Even if you see the women in his family collapse in front of him, publically, there's that clip of just both their faces like melting as he turns around, they are protected. I would use my hypnotism skills in those two minutes, to tell him 'you are a woman of color'.

AC: But what about works that you have found incredibly transformational to yourself? Or have helped you re-see something? Could you name a work?

FB: Lorna Simpson's, *Seven Day Weather Forecast.* Or Kara Walker's *Diorama Gone: An Historical Romance.* Or Goya's *Terrors.* Or the mural of the buddha at the Met–like going to a temple and seeing the human intent behind them. You see this reach for something beyond the body, beyond our present existence. Agnes Martin's rooms that are like chapels, you know? It's like this reach towards spirit, always. They're anchored in physical space but there's always a reach for something greater. But I don't think any of these ephemeral things would work with Trump.

AC: So my other question is–and I didn't even ask you what you're

Firelei Báez, Ciguapa Pantera (to all the goods and pleasures of this world), 2015, courtesy of Tiroche DeLeon Collection and Art Vantage PCC Ltd.

planning to work on for this show, which I need to ask you because it's important! But before that, what are some young artists that you're excited to see kind of blow up, that you want to namedrop right now?

FB: I'm working with some of them in this show in Ukraine. Dineo Seshee Bopape, Phoebe Boswell and Martine Syms do incredible work. And Kenny Rivero is a Dominicano around my age who makes the most sublime paintings.

AC: So what are you working on here at the Warhol?

FB: So here, we're basically continuing the premise of the Perez Exhibition–Bloodlines. Which formally traced social movements within the black diaspora in the entirety of the New World. Seeing how actions in North America, like the Harlem Renaissance or the Black Power Movement were all in conversation with movements that were happening in the Caribbean. And even if you think of North African revolutions, they were also being informed by Caribbean theory. So making concrete and obvious those interactions, down to a formal level, connecting the black power fist, the socialist fist with the figa or el azabache. At the same time as the Perez Museum of Art in Miami show there was a sister exhibition at the Utah Museum of Contemporary Art that was titled Patterns of Resistance, and this exhibition at The Warhol will be a a melding of those two.

Bamboo Wedding

Sujatha Fernandes

It was a quiet day at the admissions office at NYU. Somwattie and Devika stood at the front desk, speaking to a female administrator about Devika's acceptance to the MFA studio art program.

"You're not eligible to apply for financial aid. You're illegal," the administrator told Devika. Devika might well have had a flashing neon "I" printed on her forehead.

"What are the fees for one year's tuition?" asked Somwattie.

The officer ran her finger down a column on her paperwork. "Forty-one thousand and forty-four dollars. Then there are supplies and living expenses too."

Somwattie may have been semi-literate but she was sharp when it came to numbers, due to all her small business schemes back home in Guyana. With the total of five hundred and fifty dollars she brought home each week from six cleaning jobs, it would take her years to even earn that amount. All of her savings had gone toward putting Devika through Queens College.

"There must be some scholarship, or some way you can help us."

The administrator shrugged. "There's really nothing we can do. Without a social security number, we can't legally accept a financial aid application." Then she said, "The application for the fall semester is due in soon, but I can make an exception for you and give you until August. More time to figure something out."

They went back home to their one bedroom apartment in the Jamaica neighborhood of Queens. When Somwattie first arrived in New York with Devika, leaving behind her two older children in Guyana, they had stayed with Somwattie's aunt in Jamaica and Devika enrolled in the nearby Hillcrest High. Somwattie overstayed her tourist visa. Then they moved into their own place and Somwattie took up house cleaning to pay the bills. She liked living in Jamaica, having the convenience of West Indian stores nearby. She didn't like living among so many blacks. Most of the kids at Devika's school were black. Her daughter brought these kids home, talked like them, brash and loud. In Guyana during the sixties, Africans and Indians clashed. Somwattie said that the two races could never get along. Devika called her a racist.

Later that evening, Somwattie called up her siblings in Guyana to ask their advice.

"Why you worry?" said her brother. "She's twenty-two years old. She should be thinking about marriage."

Her sister agreed. "Don't make her wait till she's old. Her beauty is fading. Soon she'll get fat and ugly."

They didn't know that Devika wanted to be an artist. Somwattie pleaded with her daughter to apply to nursing school, something practical. But Devika spent all the money from her babysitting jobs on paint and canvases. The paintings were stacked up around their small apartment: strange pictures of severed hands, cherubic brown babies, and floating eyeballs. Somwattie felt embarrassed to invite her friends over. Her headstrong daughter insisted on applying to art school for a masters, one of the best art schools she proudly told her mother when she received the acceptance letter from NYU. But what was the use when you couldn't pay for it?

Devika lay deflated on the couch, her long black hair trailing over the pillows.

Somwattie moved a pillow and sat down next to her. "Why don't you do a course in selling real estate or life insurance? Learn some useful skills."

No response.

*

On Commencement day at Queens College, Somwattie woke up early. She eased her wide feet into a new pair of brown suede flats and brought out her dry-cleaned crimson silk blouse. She was heavyset, in an athletic, muscular way. Her hair was wispy with hints of gray and she had dark rings under her eyes, but her smile hinted at the beauty she once was.

Somwattie wanted her daughter to wear her graduation gown on the Q25 bus, despite the soaring pre-summer temperatures. She had taken on extra jobs for weeks to afford the cap and gown rental. Somwattie wanted the bus driver, the matronly older lady with a walker, and the two kids playing video games to know that she was the mother of a graduate. She fussed with her daughter's hair, arranged and rearranged the velvet collar on the gown. For once, Devika didn't complain.

The quad was still fairly empty when they arrived. Somwattie took an aisle seat. The sun beat down and she fanned herself with her folded program. Her feet felt itchy and uncomfortable in her tight new shoes. Soon the seats around her filled up with the jubilant, noisy families of graduates.

The orchestra started up a slow paced processional and the graduates began to march to the front. Somwattie looked out for her daughter until she finally came into view, her petite frame hidden beneath folds and folds of black gown, her wise eyes matched by the solemnity of her scholar's cap. Devika was an old soul. Even as a child, there was something about Devika's eyes that made Somwattie feel she had been in this world already.

Devika spotted her mother and waved. Somwattie felt her face wet. She was not a sentimental person. But she couldn't stop the tears that ran down her cheeks and left damp patches on her blouse. This girl — the granddaughter of a cane cutter — was a college graduate. Somwattie's mother had died young and her father couldn't afford to send any of his ten children to high school. They were pulled out of school one by one to help in the cane fields or be married off. And Somwattie too had put her older son and daughter to work in Guyana, earning extra money to help pay the rent and bills. But Somwattie always made sure that Devika could study. She would prepare roti, dal, chow mein, or curry chicken for her daughter, and leave her to her studies before going off to another cleaning job. She waved back at Devika. For this moment alone, it was all worth it. If her father was alive he would've been proud.

Somwattie eased her swelling feet out of her shoes. She would soak them in warm water at home. As the speaker droned on and on, Somwattie's mind started to wander. Without her papers, Devika couldn't go to art school. She couldn't even get a job that would recognize her degree. Somwattie had gone over the options endlessly in her head. She had seen the immigration lawyers' offices along Liberty Avenue. But the lawyers took hefty fees and promised nothing. She couldn't take the risk. What if they got deported? There had to be another way. After the ceremony was over, they waited on Kissena for the Q25.

"Why don't you marry for a green card?"

Devika looked aghast. "Like putting an ad in the paper and interviewing prospective husbands?"

Somwattie considered the idea briefly. "No, no. We put the word out with friends here and in Guyana. Your uncle and auntie will be pleased."

"Never. I don't want to be tied down to a deadbeat like you were."

Somwattie was quiet. "There *are* good men out there. You're a very pretty girl. Believe me, plenty of boys will be knocking on our door."

"You were married to someone who stole from you, beat you, and cheated on you until he finally left you. Now you work yourself like a dog just to pay the bills. And you want me to marry?"

Somwattie had lived a tough life, maybe it was karma. Her father – a man with a proverb for every occasion – would have said: "If you plant plantain you can't reap cassava."

Mother and daughter rode the bus together in silence. The cap and gown lay balled up in Devika's shoulder bag.

*

On Monday of the following week, Devika accompanied her mother to her cleaning job at an Upper East Side condo. Her cap and gown regalia replaced by a faded sweater and an old pair of jeans. What else was there for the girl to do?

They arrived at a building with an elaborate ornate stonework entrance. The doorman greeted them. He had a strong square jaw and dark skin, and was somewhere in his mid-twenties, his short afro covered by a black hat.

"Where's my *dhalpuri*?" There was a Caribbean lilt to his accent. He winked at Somwattie. "You know I can't let you in the building till I have my *dhalpuri*."

"You don't have no shame, you young kids," Somwattie shot back, as she brought out a plastic container of flaky flatbreads stuffed with ground up split peas. "I spent a couple well hours yesterday making these for you."

The doorman took the container. Devika cleared her throat.

"Oh, yes, this is my girl Devika. A college graduate," she added proudly. "And this is Mr. Owen."

"Pleased to meet you. A graduate, huh? What are you doing now?"

Devika looked down at her faded clothes and laughed. "Well, I'm not exactly going to work as an investment banker or corporate executive dressed like this, am I?"

"I didn't mean to…" Mr. Owen stammered.

Devika waved her hands. "No shame in cleaning houses."

*

Somwattie used her keys to open the door to the Paulson family's eighth floor apartment. She always fumbled with the high security locks designed to keep out any intruders who could make it past a twenty-four hour doorman guarded entrance.

They crossed the foyer and entered the spacious living room with white padded sofas, drooping buttercups in a vase on the coffee table, and wall to wall bookcases with more books than Somwattie supposed anyone could read in a lifetime. She was proud of the apartment. It looked this way because every week *she* vacuumed the sofas, polished the flower vases, and dusted the bookshelves.

The kitchen sink was piled with dishes from the weekend. Somwattie opened the cabinet under the sink to take out the cleaning supplies. She shook the Ajax tin, it was almost empty. Her employer had forgotten to get a new one.

Somwattie sighed and fished out a five dollar bill. "Devika, go to the supermarket on Madison and pick up a new tin of Ajax. Make sure it has bleach. And don't forget to ask for a receipt." Even Ajax was expensive around here. If it was on her dime she would try to find it on sale at Walmart or one of the 99 cent stores in her neighborhood.

After Devika left the apartment, Somwattie stopped for a moment to savor the stillness. She was accustomed to having the apartments to herself while she cleaned. It was so different to the noise and chaos of the factories where she had worked in Guyana. Clocking on. Clocking off. Sitting all day in an assembly line sticking labels on containers. Supervisors breathing down your neck telling you to work faster. No time to take bathroom breaks or have a sip of water. Here she was her own boss. No one told her what to do.

She had only met Mrs Paulson once, it was during the job interview. Mrs Paulson was a brisk, pleasant woman in her mid-forties. "Somwattie. I'll never remember that name!" she had exclaimed. "Can I call you Stephanie?"

Somwattie started in the children's bedroom. She had never met the Paulson children, but from the copious toys and clothes that she picked up every week, and the photos on the wall, they looked like they were a girl and boy about six and eight years old. There was a trail of clothing leading from the little girls' unmade pink bed to the door. The girl must have stepped right out of her underwear and pajamas as she undressed. Somwattie picked up the discarded clothes between two fingers, shaking her head. American kids didn't know how to pick up after themselves. When she was growing up in Guyana, her father would be in the fields from morning to night, and the children would have to look after each other. The oldest would feed and bathe the youngest. By the age of five or six you had to start helping your older siblings with fetching cow dung, cleaning the chicken coop, and cooking breakfast. And here a six year old couldn't even put her dirty underwear into the clothes hamper.

After she finished picking up all the toys and clothes, Somwattie vacuumed the circus elephants rug. It was hard to grow up kids in this country, she thought. You couldn't beat them. Somwattie raised three children as a single mother in Guyana because she could keep them in line. If they left underwear on the floor or threw food from their plates? Smack. And not just a dainty slap but a good resounding whack. They wouldn't do it again. Americans were too scared to hit their kids. They worried that they would damage them. And instead they made them spoiled and lazy.

Somwattie finished mopping the floor and dusting the furniture in the children's room. She looked at her watch. Forty minutes had passed. It shouldn't take so long to buy a tin of Ajax.

She started on the living room. As she bent over to pick up action figures and books from the floor she felt a sharp pain in her lower back. "Bend your knees when you pick things up. It'll put less pressure on your back," one of her employers had instructed her once. Thanks for your concern, she had thought. How about you pick up your own things, that'll put even less pressure on my back. The pain in her lower back had gotten much worse over the years. She didn't have health insurance to get x-rays or see a chiropractor, so she treated the pain herself by drinking homemade beet juice – her personal remedy for everything. And maybe one day her daughter would be a famous artist and take care of her. She could finally retire, go on one of those temple-organized trips to India to see the Ganges and the Taj Mahal.

The Paulsons were messy people, but they paid her well. The Niemanns and the Garners didn't give yearly raises or holiday bonuses. Last year, when the Niemanns went to Italy for a month, they told her they wouldn't be needing her services while away. But she had to pay her rent and bills too. She never said anything, even though Devika pushed her to. Karma comes back around.

Finally the front door opened and Devika walked in, looking flushed.

"Where were you? I thought you got lost."

"No," Devika was out of breath. "I… I just couldn't find the store. But here it is." She produced the tin.

"Ok, go start on the bathrooms. And hurry up, we don't have no time to waste."

Later that evening, Somwattie and Devika were at home in the kitchen, cleaning up after dinner. "I've been thinking about about getting married for papers?"

"Mmm hmm." Somwattie didn't look up from the pot that she was scrubbing.

"Maybe a green card marriage might be my only hope. But just for the papers. I'm not going to cook and clean for him or have babies."

Somwattie smiled into her pot. She didn't know what had produced such a sudden change of heart in Devika, but she wasn't asking.

"Fine. I'll make a few calls tomorrow." Somwattie's voice was as steady and casual as she could manage.

That same night, Somwattie got the word out with lightning speed. Even once a green card application was in, she had heard that it could take several months to get issued a social. Besides, she didn't want her daughter to change her mind. Devika had a photo taken at a studio on Hillside Avenue with a fake sky background provided by billowing tie-dyed blue bedsheets. She posed with crossed legs, her long hair pulled back in a clasp, her almond-shaped eyes serious. Somwattie shared the photo among her circle of friends.

Some weeks later, inquiries started coming in. They settled on a few prospective suitors. Somwattie wanted to set up meetings, but Devika preferred to "chat" online with them first. You can get to know them better that way, she explained. What's there to know? argued Somwattie. You see them, you like them. End of story.

As Somwattie got ready for bed, brushing her teeth and saying her prayers, she would hear the tik-tik-tik of keys as Devika chatted with her suitors. After a week, she announced that she had a date with Sonny, a cargo worker at JFK. He came over on Friday evening, an eager and skinny young man with a goatee and short spiky hair.

"Where were you born? Are your parents here in the US? What does your father do? How many years you been working at the airport?" Somwattie barraged him with questions. Devika rolled her eyes.

"How much do you earn?"

"Moooom!" Devika had enough. "What's up with all the questions?"

"Well, some of these boys, they just like plenty girls but they don't have no good prospects."

"Goodbye." Devika grabbed Sonny's arm and steered him out the door.

When Devika returned home after the date, she was coy and impenetrable. She wouldn't answer Somwattie's questions. "Are you going to meet again? Did he take you to an expensive restaurant? Do you like him?"

But as soon as Somwattie had gone to bed she heard Devika on the computer again. Tik tik tik, tik-tik-tik-tik-tik-tik. Pause. Tik-tik-tik-tik.

*

All through June, Devika accompanied Somwattie to her Monday cleaning job. The girl was a help, but she took her time getting ready: applying eyeliner and lipstick, and trying on several pairs of pants. "You don't have to nice yourself up. It's just a cleaning job." She liked to get an early start on her jobs. While cleaning, Devika would find frequent reasons to take breaks. Somwattie just shook her head. Her daughter could spend hours doodling away on those canvases, but give her some real physical work and she couldn't handle it.

On weekends, Devika went on dates with Sonny. But Sonny didn't come to the apartment anymore to pick her up. "You scared him, mom," Devika joked. Instead, they would meet for their dates in Richmond Hill or downtown Manhattan. Somwattie waited up for her daughter, scanning the passing cars for Sonny's platinum-colored Infiniti. But all she could see were the jeeps and vans of the black kids on the street, pulsating with the rowdy music they liked. Eventually she gave up, closed the windows, pulled down the shades, and went to bed, still listening for the sound of her daughter's key in the front door. Devika came home from her dates with gifts – an emerald green purse, a pretty silver bracelet, a box of Godiva chocolates.

On weeknights, Devika would stay up late chatting online, with Sonny again, Somwattie supposed. She urged Devika to set a date to get married. With less than two months to go, they had to act quickly if she wanted to get her papers in time. Devika simply smiled and told her not to worry. It drove Somwattie crazy that Devika never talked to Sonny on the phone. That way at least she could eavesdrop. But it was always the online chatting, the tik-tik-tik of computer keys. Even if Somwattie had known how to use a computer, she was not a strong reader. She had only studied up to the fifth grade, and it took effort to sound out the words, put them together into sentences.

There was no denying that the girl was happy. She smiled at Somwattie, tolerated her frequent pestering, even ate her extra spicy curry chicken without complaining. On Sunday afternoons, she painted in her room, humming a tune. When Somwattie came home after a long day, Devika had a bucket of warm water ready and she rubbed and kneaded her mother's sore feet.

Somwattie started dreaming of weddings. While at the temple in Ozone Park one Sunday, she imagined the ceremonies in detail. She wanted her daughter to have a proper bamboo wedding in traditional Hindu style. She would hire out a hall with a real maro canopy for the puja ceremonies. Only the tender young bamboo leaves and shoots were used for the maro, the overlapping sheaths forming protective layers. She would purchase the saris and jarjamas for bride and groom and prepare a banquet of potato curry, puris, dal, and spinach for cook night. No matter if she would have to do it all on short notice. It was important that this girl be married right. Somwattie couldn't marry her other two children in Guyana. Her siblings had organized their weddings a few years back. Since she had no papers, Somwattie couldn't even travel back home to attend their weddings or see the three grandchildren that she now had.

She remembered back to her own sham wedding. Her mother-in-law rubbing tumeric into her body, the ceremony barely over and her new husband back at the rumshop. No dig dutty offerings to Mother Earth or the saptapadi seven steps. Her father was not present, nor her siblings or relatives. Her father disliked the boy from the beginning because the boy's father was a drunk and they lived in a small mud floor hut. So she met with him secretly. Then one night her older sister dreamt that Somwattie was pregnant. Her sister told her father about the dream. They noticed that for two months, Somwattie had not washed and hung her menstrual cloths out to dry. Her father didn't speak to her again. On the day she left home, he was planting ochro in his little garden, his face hardened in disappointment. That was the last time she saw him alive. Her siblings summoned her many years later, on the day he lay brain-dead in the hospital.

Somwattie was leaving the temple when she saw her friend Mrs. Ramdas. Mrs. Ramdas had introduced them to Sonny. She rushed to embrace her warmly.

"It was so good of you to introduce us to Sonny, such a nice young boy. He and my daughter are to marry soon, god willing," Somwattie said.

"What are you talking about?" Mrs. Ramdas looked perplexed. "His mother told me that they only went out once and then he never heard from her again."

"But how can that be?" Somwattie's head was spinning. The dates. The chatting. The gifts.

"I'm sorry, dear. That's what his mother told me."

She couldn't believe it. Mrs. Ramdas had no proof. Anyway, Somwattie knew the youthful glow of infatuation. As she rode the bus back along Liberty Avenue, she gazed wistfully at the store-front mannequins decked out in embroidered wedding saris of gauzy crepe and red georgette.

*

On their way to the Paulson's place the next morning, Somwattie and Devika sweltered on the subway platform. It always felt ten degrees hotter on the platform than outside. When the E train arrived, Somwattie was relieved to see that the subway car in front of them looked almost empty. But once inside the air was stifling. People were melting into their plastic seats. They had boarded the one car without air conditioning. Now they would have to sit and fry like chickpeas dry roasting in a pan.

Mr. Owen was waiting outside the building when they arrived. His eyes crinkled in a smile and he opened his arms when he saw the women approach.

"My two favorite ladies," he grinned. Devika giggled.

"I brought homemade coconut rolls for you today Mr. Owen,"

Somwattie handed over a thick packet. "I grated the coconut myself."

Mr. Owen's eyes widened. He took out one of the pastries with its sweet bread and moist red coconut filling. "Thank you. I'll enjoy this at my tea break this morning." He glanced over at Devika.

"Enjoy!" said Devika extra brightly, as she pulled her mother inside.

Upstairs, Somwattie decided that they would begin cleaning in the living room. It might give her a chance to get more information from her daughter. Somwattie sprayed Windex on the glass window and rubbed away at it with some bunched up newspaper. Her eyes teared up at the fumes.

"Mom," Devika watched her. "Why do you use those strong chemicals?"

"I'm fine. I'm used to it." Somwattie continued scrubbing. "Come on, let's just do it. We'll get it done faster together."

"Not without a face mask. I'll get one at the hardware store on Madison."

Somwattie exhaled, exasperated by the girl. "Forget it! Just go dust in the bedroom," she called after Devika but the girl had already slammed the door shut on her way out.

The chemicals had affected Somwattie's eyes and skin over the years, though she wouldn't admit it to her daughter. The Windex fumes stung her eyes and the back of her throat burned as she worked. She went to the kitchen for a drink. There she noticed that water was seeping out from under the fridge and pooling around the cabinets. She quickly mopped it up and placed a few rags around the edges of the fridge and then she went to call downstairs for the super.

The intercom was in the living room. Somwattie hadn't used the device before. There were a lot of buttons. She mistakenly pressed one that was marked "listen" and suddenly her daughter's laughter floated up through the speaker.

Why don't you wear the red blouse I bought for you when we go out this weekend? I want to see it on you.

Where are we going? To another party?

I thought we might go to the Nicki Minaj show.

Somwattie's hand was shaking as she pressed the "speak" button.

"Mr. Owen, send my daughter upstairs. Right. Now."

Devika's eyes were defiant as she walked into the living room.

"You…you… lied to me," Somwattie said, stuttering, her face hot.

"How could I say anything?"

Somwattie scrubbed the window furiously with the newspaper. "So are you in love with Mr. Owen, the doorman?"

"We've only been dating for a month. But I like him a lot. And he understands my situation. He's willing to help me get my green card."

Somwattie didn't reply. Devika picked up a Swiffer duster and started dusting the bookcases.

"You can't marry him."

"Why not?" Devika looked her mother in the eye. "You know Owen. You like him. You cook food for him. What's the problem, mom?"

Somwattie sprayed more Windex on the window pane. "He's black."

"Yeah, he's black, so what? According to you, all black people are violent thugs and freeloaders. Well, news flash, mom. Dad was all those things. And he was Indian."

Somwattie reached for some fresh newspaper and scrunched it up with her hands. "Devika, you don't understand. You don't know what happened during the riots. The black men raping Indian girls. Killing Indian children."

"But Owen's not even Guyanese. He's a Trini! What does he have to do with riots and children being killed?" Devika stabbed at the top of the books with her duster.

Somwattie gathered the pile of soiled bunched up newspapers. They left smudged black print on her palms. Her eyes were red and irritated. "Well, Mr. Owen is not a Hindu," she said, weakly. "You can't have a bamboo wedding."

Devika put down the duster. She reminded her mother that this whole plan was *her* idea, a way to get a green card and go to art school. It was never about having a traditional bamboo wedding.

Somwattie kept her voice low. She didn't want the neighbors to hear them arguing and report it to the Paulsons. "This plan was a bad idea," she said. "You don't want to marry someone just for a piece of paper because then you're stuck with that person forever. I married a sweet-skin, good-for-nothing man because I got pregnant and see how much I've suffered. I don't want you to suffer too."

Devika sat and held her face in her palms. "Owen is not Dad. He's nothing like Dad."

Somwattie turned quietly back to her work. Devika would forget about Mr. Owen soon enough. And maybe there would still be time to contact the lawyers, enter a green card lottery, find a relative willing to sponsor her. Anything but this.

*

Somwattie and Devika didn't speak much that evening. After dinner, Devika picked up the phone to call Owen. No more tik-tik-tik of the computer keys. There was nothing to hide now. Somwattie stuck her head in the fridge and pretended to sort through last week's leftovers. Devika held her hand over the receiver. "Mom, can I get some privacy?"

Somwattie nodded reluctantly and went into the bedroom, shut the door. She fought the urge to pick up the other receiver and listen in, it would be too obvious. She settled for putting her ear to the door. She could make out a few fragments, the low buzz of conversation occasionally transmuted into patches of phrases.

"...happened so quickly...we're young..."

Devika's voice was muffled and Somwattie strained to hear. She blocked her other ear and concentrated hard on what her daughter was saying.

"...just to get into art school...rushing things"

"...see each other...don't care...be together..." Then there was an airplane cruising overhead and police sirens and Somwattie couldn't make out anything else.

*

In early September, the final letter came from NYU. Somwattie brought the mail on her way in from a long day with two back-to-back cleaning jobs. Her daughter was out at a babysitting job. She opened the envelope. "We regret to inform you that NYU has offered our position to one of the candidates on the waiting list. We wish you good luck with your future endeavors." She tore up the letter, first into big pieces, and then smaller and smaller pieces. No art school. No bamboo wedding. And her daughter dating a black man. She didn't blame anyone but herself. There was no getting away from one's misdeeds in the past. The thought provided her some relief. She didn't have to struggle anymore. She put her tired feet up on the couch and closed her eyes.

As she reclined, she felt a figure hovering above her. It was feminine, but she knew it was her father. She could tell by the faint smell of hospital disinfectant. She heard a cough in her ear, and then felt a light pressure on her shoulder. She reached out with her arms, wanting to grasp him, to ask if he regretted turning her out, if he had missed her. But he was gone just as quickly as he had appeared. She smiled faintly, rubbing her shoulder as if to connect with his touch. Then she slipped into a sweet dream where she was a little girl again, playing on the floor while her father made sugar cakes. She felt good here, in her innocence, in her father's love.

What We Know About Men

Isobel O'Hare

1. Harvey Weinstein
2. Louis C.K.
3. Kevin Spacey
4. Richard Dreyfuss
5. George Takei
6. Jeremy Piven

I came of age in
culture
of
demons
I
respect
more
tha
n
women

my dick
is a question
I
run from

there are stories out there about me
that
have
been fueled by
my
own behavior.
- Kevin Spacey
Kevin Spacey
@KevinSpacey

Isobel O'Hare

George Takei
Friends,
you
do not
know me
and
I
cannot tell you
to
trust
me
George

these women
destroy careers
and need to be addressed
- Jeremy Piven
Jeremy Piven
@jeremypiven

It's been three months since the last drop of rain

Rina Garcia Chua

I.

the seagulls circle the empty
parking lot, thinking gravel
can melt into liquid

a thin squirrel carries a dry
nut across the field, its body
crouching in greed

grass has become painfully
dry – paper brown silhouettes
sticking up to the heat

noisy magpies peck at food
forgotten on the courtyard;
sneering at the shiny ravens

II.

my skin is mutinous, lost
in a terrene that it has never

thought existed

it lusts for the nine days of
drought, and nine days of
water, so much water

which cleansed stray dogs
on the street; once, I saw them
swim in the flood

the yowling cats were quieted,
their arrogance stomped on by
the thunderstorms

and the maya birds, when light
seeped through banana trees,
sang from their bellies

III.

yet, when the clouds roared
and gaped at our thirst, they
unleashed a familiar rhythm

it doesn't change – the scent
of the land's exhale when it again
tastes the tang of rain

that first drip on the arid grass
still brings the birds to sing, and
when I close my eyes, I'm certain

that no time has passed. My skin
has stretched across an ocean
and I'm here and there, both.

Turning

Rina Garcia Chua

Orchards scrape putrid
fruits from dehydrated
trees. Smoke won't let up –
the sun fashions an eerie
orange eye.

Fruit flies buzz outside
buildings, stick to sweaty
skins. A fat one slithered
in my room; not even
the cat paws it.

My eyes water, a remnant
of the Pisces moon, or perhaps
the Valley is finally getting to me.
My chest hums, an overinflated
balloon –

I have yet to sleep since
the morning you left
rest is possible only when
I can again see mountains.

The next fire may be too close
and the sirens keep me awake
I fear waking up in a bed of flames,
this same bed, no way out,
begging to see you one last time.

I still have everything here,
except for you. Haze
persists and the sun
raptures, but there we'll
be above all ruin –
sharing sunsets, kissing
in woods, picking cherries.

Native Tongue

Ola Osifo Osaze

It was the summer of 2010 at the height of World Cup fever on an unusually slow afternoon at Festac Grill, a Nigerian restaurant sandwiched between an empty lot strewn with refuse and a car repair shop. This working-class Brooklyn neighborhood, whose streets were desolate at night, was busy during the day. At the repair shop, Black and brown men in blue overalls peered into hoods of cars and slid underneath them to poke at their bellies. A man and I were waiting for our takeout at the food counter in the dim restaurant. Its peach-colored walls were lined with haunting carved wood masks and canvasses drenched in vivid hues of blues, reds, and yellows. The aroma of goat meat pepper soup and ogbono thickened the air. Through tall black speakers sequestered in the corners of the oblong room, 9ice serenaded us with *Mu Number*. On one side of the room, mounted at the center of the wall, was a giant flat screen TV on which a soccer match was live: Senegal vs USA. A few male patrons sat facing the screen with fingers poised in midair clasping soup-soaked balls of iyan.

"Ah ah! He should have scored, abi?" said one of them, dark like me.

The thin man beside me whose walnut brown face was all angles and stubble, wondered why our country, with all the skill we could boast of, was yet to take home the Cup. Our conversation began in pidgin, inflected with more and more Yoruba. Eventually, no longer capable of continuing the charade, I told him I didn't speak the language.

Sometimes the exchange of hellos, of names, of places of birth would be enough to establish my Nigerian authenticity and bring these exchanges, these brief moments of recognition and connection, to a close. At other times, they were merely the ice-breaker; as people would launch into more complicated phrases, the singsong dialect pouring out of their mouths rapidly, my lack of fluency would become evident and my long-held shame would manifest a grim smile. I'm almost forty now, practically middle-aged, and still that grim smile is the best I can do when reminded of this cultural failing, this foreign-ness of my own native tongue.

"What do you mean you don't speak Yoruba," he asked, a shadow of pity darkening his face. "You should know how to speak your language. Didn't your parents speak it at home?"

He raised an incredulous eyebrow and rested his hand on the counter. When I didn't answer right away, he turned to face me and got a good look at the Yoruba and Edo kid who could barely carry on a conversation in either language. I did not know what to say to him: Do I say what I usually said, that, yes, my parents spoke multiple languages at home, but only to each other and not to us kids? That we were discouraged from speaking our languages? That we were discouraged from even speaking pidgin because, according to them, "that's how bush people communicate"? Do I talk about how, despite spending the first fifteen years of my life in Nigeria, I barely knew the place? That during that time, when I wasn't away at boarding school, I only ever saw the compounds of our homes, the interiors of our chauffeured cars? Do I tell him about the vice-like grip our parents, particularly my mom, had on us, and the paranoia undergirding it?

"No, I don't speak Yoruba."

The man shook his head, his pity looking more like sorrow. He grabbed his plastic bag—in which there were tupperwares containing fufu and egusi—off the counter and sauntered out of the restaurant. I looked at the woman at the cash register. Her ponytail was slowly coming undone and sweat beaded down her caramel forehead. Just beyond her was the kitchen where, through the glass panel of the door, I could see two older women in head ties, bent over the sink washing something. The cashier placed a bag of tupperware filled with my goodies on the countertop. I felt certain that she was silently judging me.

"$14.62 please?" she said.

Her eyes seemed to ask me the same questions the man had. I stared back for one second, trying to summon an unashamedness I did not feel. Failing, I lowered my gaze and fished money out of my pocket to pay her.

Yoruba, the language of my father's people who are from the western region of Nigeria, is spoken by more than twenty-two million people within Nigeria and in other countries from Benin to Brazil. This language—spoken by the people in his village of Saki and those of Lagos, Oyo, Ogun, and other Yoruba states in Nigeria—is part of the Niger-Congo group of dialects. My mother's people are from Edo state in southwestern Nigeria. They are a people who can trace their lineage back thousands of years, a people that used to be called Igodomigodos, before being renamed the Edos by Oba (the Edo word for 'King') Eweka I. Their language, also called Edo, is of the Volta–Niger subgroup of languages also within the Niger-Congo family. Edo and Yoruba, two languages that should be as familiar to me as my name, yet they are not.

The eyes through which I see the world, my habits of thought, and the languages with which I dialogue with the world are an amalgamation of my parents' ethnic and personal histories and a reality which mandated that English take precedence in our household. Though I was born in Port Harcourt, my family bounced around a lot during my childhood. Through all these geographic changes, the one constant was language; between my parents and their children, that language was English.

I spent much of my time in Port Harcourt, a city of thousands of ethnic groups and tens of thousands of expatriates. Two worlds collided in my home. In one, we were similar to an aristocratic British family where children were banished from the dining table for such atrocities as holding the fork in the right hand instead of the left or resting elbows on the dining table while eating, and good little girls, such as I was supposed to be, curtseyed or prostrated themselves when they greeted their elders. Good little children, such as I was instructed to be, only played with other good little children of similar or higher socioeconomic status. You said "yes, please" and "no thank you," not because of an inviolable respect and reverence for others, but because "that's how high-class people address each other." You were admonished if you didn't speak the Queen's English. Beethoven, Michael Jackson, ABBA, and Madonna comprised the soundtrack of our lives, instead of King Sunny Adé, Brenda Fassie, Tshala Muana, or Fela Kuti. Absent from our library were any books about Pan-Africanist movements and liberation struggles. Bleaching creams were stacked on dressing tables as part of an ongoing battle waged against encroaching blackness, which also included staying out of the sun and doing all manners of things to rid ourselves of the natural kinks in our hair.

Ours was a world riddled with the persistent fear that our wealth invited the envy of all around us, and their envy brought with it untold threats and made others dangerous and unpredictable. Mother, the perpetual worrier and the one, being a woman, with the responsibility of maintaining our household, was also the steward of this wealth, her wary eyes always surveying our surroundings for danger. Any harm that befell us, the children, reflected badly on mother and spoiled her standing in the rigid social class strata in which we found ourselves.

"Don't eat when we get to the Obbot's house. Those bush people are so jealous of us they will poison us," she would caution, with fire in her eyes.

"I don't ever want to catch you playing with Idemudia. He's below our class," she warned about my close friend in primary school.

But it was never just Idemudia or the Obbots. It was also the Osas, the Ntuens, and many others, some of whom lived as comfortably as we did. All were suspect because in Nigeria "man must wack." A person must survive at any cost.

*

Omniglot.com tells me "Yoruba" is spelled like so: Yorùbá. From Genii Games' Yoruba 101 app, I learn that the Yoruba Alufabẹẹti is comprised of twenty-five letters, though Omniglot disagrees, stating there's a twenty-sixth. The alphabet contains letters familiar to English speakers and some that are not:

"G" (sounds like "ghee") exists as does "Gb", which is a difficult sound to describe phonetically. "O" and "Ọ", with the former sounding like "oh" while the latter is pronounced like "uh".

"S" is distinct from "Ṣ", with the latter sounding like "shhh".

Of all twenty-five (or twenty-six) my favorites by far are "gb" and "kp" because of how one has to say the first letter-sound in the hollow of your throat then roll that sound into the utterance of the second letter-sound.

"Gb" sounds like the echoing of a drumbeat, while "kp" sounds like reverberating cymbals.

When I run into Yoruba people on the streets of New York where I live or in the Nigerian restaurants dotting the city, they greet me in my language.

"Bawo ni?"

With great pride I utter the correct response memorized from the recent Yoruba language website I was poring over.

"Mo wa daadaa, o̩ se."

Sometimes they ask me my name.

"Ki ni orukọ rẹ?" and I am ready with the apt response.

"Mi ni —."

Wanting to know just what type of Yoruba I am, they ask where I'm from. "Nibo ni o ti wa?"

I stumble over my answer.

"Lati Oyo State," is how I eventually respond even though Oyo State only speaks to half of my lineage. The other half, the maternal part is Edo, but Nigeria is a patrilineal society and I've grown used to saying Oyo first and Edo second, if I bring up the second at all.

For me, the inability to speak the language of my people represents the distance between the Nigeria I was taught to see and the one I want to see.

The Nigeria I was taught to see was one that was out to get us.

It was the world just beyond our tall cement fence, capped with sharp shards of green and brown glass. The Nigeria I'd love to see? One in which I maneuver the streets of Port Harcourt, Lagos, Ibadan, and other cities using the languages my ancestors inherited from my ancestors. One where I can say with the wisdom and instincts of someone enjoying the familiarity of home:

"You know that marketplace by…?"

Or

"I remember that bookstore next to the…"

Or

"I miss that buka on that street where we used to…"

The Nigeria I was taught to see was one of oil, of "how much" and "dash."

Father was the Managing Director of the Nigerian National Petroleum Corporation—the largest oil corporation in Nigeria at the time—in Port Harcourt. Mom owned many entrepreneurial ventures, like her Hotel Mona Lisa, one in Port Harcourt and another in Warri, both catering to the German, Lebanese, British, French, American oil expats and aspiring ogas. In contrast to our relatives visiting from the village or the so-called family friends whom mom regarded with suspicious looks, these expats were treated to our suya and our stout, and allowed to sit on the plush green sofa in our second living room — the one reserved for "distinguished" guests, people like Chief Fawehinmi, who, every time he arrived in his gleaming black Benz, clad in a flowing brocade agbada, was accompanied by a fair-haired European, an air of entitlement wafting in with them.

Afterwards, the guests would scurry away in the aftermath of a brokered business deal. Mom and dad would retreat into their haven where the second world in our household commenced. Here, the lingua franca was not English. Here dad's Yoruba met mom's Edo, their mingling sounds a symphony of heavy consonants and long vowels. On a bad day, which was most days of their marriage, these sounds clashed and rang through our household. They fought in these languages. They shared secrets through them and locked us out of their esoteric world.

As a child, I never questioned the predominance of English in our home. After all, the same values were reflected in every aspect of Nigerian society including schools, media, government, film, literature, workplaces, and in everyday interactions with strangers on the streets, market places, offices, and so on. The languages we were taught in school were typically French (or Latin in father's time), not even Edo or Igbo or Hausa or Ibibio or Yoruba or any one of the more than five hundred languages my people speak. Because of this nationwide complicity in the denial and relinquishing of our mother tongues, I can't blame my parents for their choices.

Father had the backbreaking pressures of being the first member of his family to go to school.

"To get there I had to travel very far. Sometimes I had to swim there," was the story he'd often tell. "But my father wanted me to go. He wanted a better life for me and he wanted me to make a better life possible for the rest of the family, which is why I didn't have to work on the farm like my brothers and sisters did."

With the benefit of an academic scholarship, he left Nigeria in the 1960s, swapping a newly independent country on the verge of a civil war for its colonial master, Britain. In black and white pictures of him prior to his emigration, father's slanted tribal marks shone, his cheeks and chin were always clean-shaven, and a shy smile lifted the corners of his lips. The pictures he later took in Birmingham showed a sullen man, his beard covering up those marks that linked him with his people. His small awkward smile only ever appeared in photographs when we were also with him.

Even after returning to Nigeria in the 1970s and ascending the ladder of oil-fueled success, he never shaved his beard again, never revealed the patterns his father, a Sango Priest, had etched into his cheeks and packed full of herbs while chanting prayers for his success.

"You don't know how good you have it," mom always said to us.

She'd regale us with stories about being poor, about the father that stood in the way of her education, about traveling far from home to somewhere in Igboland to serve as a housegirl for another family. She made it to the UK somehow—we were never told how—only to be looked down upon by the whites there, only to experience the type of poverty that forced her to eat canned cat food because it was all she could afford. By the time she met my dad at a student dance in Birmingham, rage had hardened her.

"You have to be better than them, always," she'd say to us in the rare moments when she wasn't screaming at us or beating us.

"Them" meaning white people.

"Better than" meaning mastering things like English at the expense of our own languages.

It was in search of the better-than life that my mother brought me to America in 1991. I spent a portion of my first year in a strict Christian high-school in High Point, North Carolina. There were white students everywhere. The principal mistook my Nigerian accent for a symptom of deficient mental capacity and decided to hold me back a year, so into the tenth grade I went. It was on the day we started reading Hamlet when I discovered that those white kids had a mangled grasp of the English language, that Africans were being forced to place a higher premium on the language than these people whose lips were fashioned to utter it in the first damn place.

"What does it mean, Ms. Eubanks?" the students cried out, befuddled to the point of frustration, biting their tongues and cheeks in vain attempts to read the dialogue aloud. With a smirk on my face, I showed them how. The only foreigner in that all-white class and I was more adept at the language than they were. But inevitably, every day after school I came home to a mom who roared into the phone in Edo or Yoruba, her words colliding one into another at rapid pace and not one of them meaning anything to me.

I can recognize this concerto of hard and soft tones anywhere. I've heard it float above the din of noise on Harlem's 125th street in the height of summer and the force of recognition has stopped me mid-stride. I've heard it behind me at the vegetable aisle of the grocery store and whirled around to find a full-bellied, head-tied, round-faced, cocoa-brown woman picking her way through a pyramid of navel oranges, chattering away, regaling the person on the other side of the phone with stories in Yoruba. The gb, kp, and eh sounds, even though I don't always know what the words they form mean, as familiar to me as air.

After twenty-four years in the U.S., I realize my parents were right: speaking English fluently is the cultural capital that, in a lot of ways, has made my economic survival possible. When I was undocumented, it meant I could pass as an American and, especially in the years after 9/11, made finding employment possible. Speaking English fluently gained me access to middle- and upper- middle class circles, and helped me navigate the interlocking worlds of academic, leftist, activist, and white spaces with relative ease.

Yet my parents were also very wrong: not knowing my languages is erasure, a symptom and manifestation of white supremacy. It is a continuation of the pillaging the British began in my homeland many years ago, when they named it Nigeria and attempted to subjugate the people, eradicate our cultures, and invisibilize our histories. As much as I possess a mix of English register and language that enables access into various spaces, I long for Yoruba and Edo, the familial ways of speaking for which I lack the words.

Today I am an embodiment of myriad tongues.

In my everyday life, I speak the English the Brits brought to Nigeria, the English of the African immigrant on U.S. soil that alternates between rolling Rs and hard Ts ('water' versus 'warra'), the pidgin English that is a marriage between our native tongues, urban slang and a deconstructed English, and the little bit of Yoruba and Edo I'm picking up from websites and apps. How I employ these languages of course depends on the setting.

With my Naija friends, with whom I'm usually more at ease, pidgin flows out of me unhindered:

"How body?"

"Body dey inside cloth." "You dey see am?"

"I dey see but I no 'gree. Story don get k-leg, abi?" "I no know wetin do am O. Mumu" [sucks teeth]

Speaking with co-workers—who, given the relatively few African immigrants in the U.S. nonprofit world, are usually not African—my language is American English all the way. This never feels completely comfortable. Yet I've had over two decades of practice:

"Hey there! How's it going?" "I'm doing alright."

"Did you see that post last night?"

"Yep! And I disagree completely. The author doesn't know what they're talking about."

Speaking with my best friend means we blend Urban English, and three different types of patois—Hawaiian, Japanese and Nigerian—creating a whole new dialect in the process:

"'Sup"

"Not much."

"Aiyah! Can you believe that shit? I read it and I just wanted to maka."

"Wahala. I dunno wetin dat person was thinking posting such ridiculousness. Onuku!"

With a rich donor—whose generosity is the life-blood of the nonprofit I work for—the formal politeness and aristocratic good manners my mama taught me informs my speech:

"Good to see you again!"

"You as well. How have you been?"

"I have been well. Thank you for asking!"

"I have been meaning to check in with you about the confusing post I read on my feed last night." "Yes, Mr. —, I am so glad you brought that up. Please rest assured, it is completely inaccurate and we are dealing with it."

"Oh what a relief!"

In the years since my interaction with the man at Festac Grill, I've been teaching myself my languages gradually. What I do know is how easily the words roll off my tongue, how deeply soothing it is to pronounce them:

Ẹ ku abọ Vbèè óye hé? Ẹ ku aarọ

O ye mi

Kpẹlẹ

Koyo

I say these words to dig deeper into who I am, a child of the red soil of Benin, the grey mountains of Saki, and the ocean city of Port Harcourt. These Edo-Yoruba words ground my shaky identification with the country into which I was born yet still barely know. They allow me to picture a different life for myself, one in which we kids were granted access into our parents' polyglot world, and where at night I dream in Edo and during the day—one day—I write in Yoruba.

Preferences

Amina Gautier

Jamie wakes in a bed that is not her own. It is Mikhail's bed and Mikhail's cramped apartment and tonight is the first night she has ever heard of this name attached to someone young, attractive and American, rather than old, political and Russian. Mikhail is a grad student at her university, but he is not her T.A. and they are not on-campus, so it is all right.

He has taken her to his place in one of the nearby towns whose name she always forgets. It is either Mountain View or Menlo Park, depending on which way they headed on El Camino.

Drinks in his apartment, seated on his floor near his couch, her back against his chest, his legs on either side of hers, comfortable. Mikhail says he went to the party "on a lark" and she finds the phrase expressive, charming. Jamie is a smart girl, capable of appreciating irony.

Mikhail has no television. Planks of wood balanced on cinder blocks serve as bookshelves. There are more books than shelves to hold them. Books are stacked haphazardly atop each other, splayed open. More than a few are upside down. His many books are haggard with wear and tear. Even from her seat on the floor, she can see the violence that's been done to them. She thought a grad student would have been gentler.

He offers her a back rub.

How easy and innocent it all begins. Thumbs kneading shoulders, pads of flesh digging into skin. A simple whispered question, "Wanna come with me to the back room?"

The moment is so similar to the one earlier in the evening when–her back braced against the wall and his hands nestled in the back pockets of her jeans– Mikhail nuzzled her and said, "Do you want go somewhere and maybe have a drink or two?"

She appreciates the way he says *back room* instead of bedroom as if he is inviting her to view a painting and not asking to get lucky. She has already gone this far, but there is a certain point beyond which she will not go. By this far, she means coming to his place. She has no intention of sleeping with him, however, and to enter his bedroom would make him think otherwise. As though the events of the early evening were not meant to lead up to this, she turns to face him and says, "I would prefer not to."

It sounds more prim than she would like, a guest declining the last deviled egg on a bed of lettuce.

He stops rubbing.

"This is too much like high school," Mikhail says without rancor, meaning she is too much like high school. Implying he's been mistaken in her. She isn't, after all, astute enough, modern enough, progressive enough, mature enough.

She is silent. Stiffly, she scoots away from him until her back touches the wall.

On hands and knees he crawls across the carpet to her. "Look," he says. "I'm sorry. I didn't mean it like that."

"It's okay," she mumbles, unwilling to let him know he's hurt her. She smiles weakly to let him see she is not accusing. She is unsurprised when he kisses her; she thinks it's his way of apologizing.

*

Her clothing does not come off, but articles of clothing are unbuttoned, unzipped, and unfastened. She is askew beneath him on the carpet, covered by his body, pinned by his weight and entangled by his limbs. There is no more kissing, no more rubbing. She is splayed like one of the books on his shelves, handled none too gently. She thinks he mistakes her shaking her head, her resistance, her pushing against him for something else though what the something else could be she doesn't know.

*

Afterwards.

"May I use your bathroom?"

Without opening his eyes, Mikhail points down the hall.

In Mikhail's bathroom, there is only one wash cloth and bath towel on the rack. No hand towels for guests. Jamie rinses his bar of soap under hot water, then washes her face with her hands. She dries her hands on his towel, seeing the black smudge on her hand, a left over from the party. They'd marked an X on her hand in magic marker so she could reenter the student center at will. At Orientation, they warn you about what can happen at a party, what can happen on a date. But she was no longer at the party and she and Mikhail weren't actually on a date. Technically, tonight counts as nothing. Tonight does not exist.

She feels too tired to go back out to Mikhail's living room. Too tired to see him. Too tired to think. She goes further down the hallway to his bedroom, where she had not wanted to go before, and curls up on top of his covers. It no longer matters if she is back here.

*

Sometime later he wakes her and says, "Think I should take you home now."

Jamie rises silently, wordlessly reaching for the thin jacket he's holding for her. Without his help, she slips herself into it and follows him out.

Mikhail opens the car door for her. He asks if she is hungry, if she wants to grab a bite to eat at either Denny's or Jack in the Box, the only two near things open this time of night.

"I'm not hungry."

"Sure?" he asks, belatedly solicitous. "It's no trouble. They're both on the way."

"I would prefer not to," she says, wanting only to go 'home'—which is how she thinks of her dorm on campus— to her own bed, her own wash cloth and her own bath towel, folding her hands in her lap and looking ahead on El Camino at the oncoming cars with their bright lights winking as if they know her.

Lost the Root

Isabel Acevedo

Spirit, grow like flamboyán, a blaze
blooming red. Everything red.
Black and brown, mancha
de plátano—I can't see it now.
Come back to me, Isla,

that I might taste you in the gradation
flesh of a mango. Flicker in the mauve
moon freckled water. Call to me
in the salted blue mouth, call

in the swinging
creaks of coquí on the tree bark.
Rise from your green ripple
mountains. Raise me.

The World We Choose, the World We Love

Michelle Yasmine Valladares

for Nicole Kaltz

Pears ripen. The turtle crosses
a walking path to her nesting ground.
My dog attacks her own shadow.

Lily pads cover the lake,
rise from the muck
of fallen trunks and storm

debris. Green algae thick
on the pond. Early
summer and it is cool.

In San Miguel my sweet
girl is dying of cancer.
The wall built between Tijuana

and San Diego extends into
the Pacific. Deported
mothers kept from their babies

by finger-thick slats, use
fingers, *Kissing fingers*
for *te amo—te echo de menos.*

A sparrow has a dirt bath
and the bottlebrush buckeye
blossoms stand upright

like drill sergeants
instructing the clouds
and sun. Monarchs

appear among the white
and yellow butterflies
in the rain garden.

A praying mantis wavers
on a blade of grass. The cornelian
cherry drops its fruit

in the small palms
of children as offerings.
Aspen branches rustle

in the wind, remind
us of a heaven
we stopped believing.

But our burning world
in your thin arms

is the same one we choose
to practice love in.

Dao Strom in Conversation

Vi Khi Nao

Where do I begin to introduce you to Dao Strom? Do I begin with her seduction with sound? The sultry provocation with her own vocal cord or instrumental cord, let's say guitar? Or her irresistible, indestructible arrangement of images? Is Dao Strom an architect of image, word, sound? She is a poet, but you will find quickly that the Buddhism or monotheism or spinal cord of that word is limiting. As you enter the pages of her intoxicating bilingual poetry collection from Ajar: *You Will Always Be Someone From Somewhere Else*, you will discover, as I have discovered, that the slow, seductive music of her polychromatic creativity and her diverse artistic longing are arranged with the seas in mind: sea of unity, sea of separation, sea of disruption, sea of departure, sea of "not here, not here," sea of space and more space, sea of white pages, and sea of cannot, sea of silence, sea of insulation, sea of insinuation, sea of nonfiction, sea of history, sea of loneliness and sea of solitude.

You will notice the dexterity of her art, how she is willing to use everything (poetry, art, memories, travelogue, photography, image art, piano, bells, harmonies, acoustic and electric cities of words to create a language that is geographically symmetrical to her heart and tongue and where the mind can memorize, but cannot pinpoint or pigeonhole. Her beautiful work from Ajar moves like a decapod: organic and it flows. Or, after you depart from the cinema of her sea, you may ask, what or who is she? And, why is she able to dismantle my soul so easily? With a few gestures of her aching voice, aching image, aching language? Aching structure of irrepressible beauty? And, the breathtaking landscape of distilled despair. And, how is she able to make desolation so compellingly hospitable? What is her secret?

When you encounter her work on a macro scale, outside of her poetry collection from Ajar, a bilingual press based in Ha Noi, and spearheaded by two brave women, into the impartial void of her entire work as deeply presented to you on her website, you feel that sound and image are individualistic in themselves, distinguished from one another, like a clover from a spade, but they are also unreasonably interchangeable. For certain, her beautiful work across all genres creates a nomadic, pluralistic residence in my heart where I ache each time I read her work and listen to her sing her songs. She is a filmmaker, poet, photographer, songwriter, performance artist, Vietnamese American, and so much more. The substance of who she is in this chaotic world exists in her unlimited ability to measure timelessness with her art. I ache each time I visit an image she has so diligently and tenderly placed on the alcove of her existence. I ache each time I visit her website.

I write this because the interview between me and Dao is more or less rational-based. Which is to say that you will get to see an extension of her insatiable mind. As you explore the thoughtful, deftly responses from her, you will realize that she is no onion, where if you peel one layer, another layer of her will be revealed, and then you will discover by the end of your onion journey, there is no more layer of her to peel. She is, to me, an eggplant – nightshade, peel-able without an end, and purple and oval like the vastness of our universe. Our interview may be designed to introduce and welcome you to her *You Will Always Be Someone From Somewhere Else*. However, I feel it's closer to a cough or a sneeze or one hiccup that may or may not go away. Regardless, I am privileged to have this great opportunity to invite you into her captivating world, where you are lured into being worshipped and worshipper.

You can find the vastness of her creative brilliance and allureness here: https://www.daostrom.com/

Be sure to begin with her East/West. Like this interview between Dao and me; she writes, "These songs cross countries and cultures." Dao's voice is sad, like her poetry, filled with nostalgic debris and human rind and it liberates the space of your consciousness and heart in ways you can define your artistic self and purpose by existing more with her.

*

VI KHI NAO: You are in Paris, yes?

DAO STROM: Hi Vi, yes but actually I am in Corsica at the moment, retreating in a house by the sea with 8 women writers of the Vietnamese diaspora – we are part of a collective project called She Who Has No Master(s). This collective formed to explore dialoguing, collaborating, and sharing, as Vietnamese diasporic writers, across borders. In our gathering here in Corsica, we have mostly Viet-American writers, but also one poet from Canada, and one French-Vietnamese author.

VKN: You are somewhere beautiful says Ana Božičević. She says Corsica is in Greece?

DS: I'm told it is technically a part of France, but used to be part of Italy (was colonized by France). For periods of time, the Corsicans were very resistant, forming independence movements, I hear… It is an island, on the Mediterranean, and maybe suitable as a place between places, for this gathering…

VKN: I am trying to imagine you, where you are geographically. I realized that geography isn't my strong point. I will pretend that you are married to a space that looks like sylph or a hummingbird. Thank you for enlightening me, Dao!

DS: It is in the south of France… I like the idea of thinking of it as a space (and I just looked up the word sylph). Yes – the light has a special quality here. Isa (one of our group) said the boulders by the ocean have "no nation." So maybe we are searching for geographies, for landscapes, where we can — at least for moments — blur our sense of borders and definitions. (Self-definitions, especially, too perhaps)…

VKN: Yes, self-definitions. I like that. I slept poorly for the first time in months and my mind isn't as sharp or pliable or as whetted like a bamboo…

DS: That is ok…! Ask anything you feel like, I will adapt.

VKN: You sew the narrative of your poetry with the panels and sometimes hemlines of photography. Could you tell us where your passion for photography and poetry begin? Did they happen at the same time?

DS: It has been a long road, let's see… I have always been a writer, since I was a child, stories and (written) language were places of refuge and expression for me. But then I went to college and studied filmmaking (in SF) and that is where I first began to play with the visual mediums.

Filmmaking taught me how to be very technical, I suppose, about the creative process of creating worlds, characters, stories; I had to think very pragmatically about creating shots and how to manipulate objects in an image. I eventually went to an MFA writing program and gave up on filmmaking, but the visual sense stayed with me. And eventually returned and began to influence the way I thought about words and images on the page, too.

VKN: How long did it take you to compose *You Will Always Be Someone From Somewhere Else*? The book feels infinite to me, but also, like a silent, elliptical cinema with alternating frames of light and darkness as if you are teaching us about movement of identity and movement of history slowly one page at a time.

DS: That is a nice way of describing it, thank you. These pieces were composed in the wake of my previous book, *We Were Meant To Be a Gentle People*, which is also a hybrid of image-text (and music), a project that took me a good 7 years to find my way through… In the making of that project, I *found* my form, in the sense that I found the mode(s) I needed to express the different "voices" — or mediums — I felt inclined toward using. *You Will Always Be Someone From Somewhere Else* was composed (rather quickly, in the months of March/April) using outtakes and out-growths (…) from that previous project. The images with wings are from travels in Vietnam and some from the Pacific coast, too.

VKN: The latter of my life I grew up surrounded by white people and for a long time and this may sound crazy or even absurd, but I didn't think Vietnamese people made art, create visual or intellectual or emotional things, or write poetry in the United States. They did make art, but it was elsewhere. When I heard writers such as "Stacey Tran" or

"Monique Tran" or "Le Thi Diem Thuy" or "Ocean Vuong"—I thought they were concepts created by white people to invite me to connect to another anthropological, fictional, or Martian fragment of the US. I get the sense that you were able to create more natural, creative connections with other Vietnamese? I am just beginning to understand this new language. What it is like to be well-versed in this?

DS: It's so interesting that you see me as well-versed or connected to other Vietnamese… In all honesty, I have long felt very disconnected. I also grew up surrounded by white people (small rural town, very conservative, white stepfather), and I don't speak or understand the Vietnamese language. A lot of my work as an artist has stemmed out of this sense of disconnect, perhaps too out of the sorrow/lament of it, of feeling like I don't — and cannot — ever fully belong to where I am, nor where I came from. My sense of displacement in the world has always been quite strong. I can connect this to some fundamental aspect of being, but I also see that it has quite logical ties to history — to Vietnam, the exodus, the trauma of war and its invisible echoes… It may've been in 2003, when my first book came out (the same year Monique Truong and le thi diem thuy also published their first novels), that I really first began to meet other Vietnamese American writers. I was invited by Isabelle Thuy Pelaud, co-founder (with Viet Thanh Nguyen) of Diasporic Vietnamese Artists Network, dvan.org, to a reading event in San Francisco that featured Vietnamese diasporic artists, including writers like Monique and Thuy, too. Over the years since, I've developed a relationship with DVAN, and their related blog, diacritics.org. Along with Isabelle and other women writers, in 2015 we initiated the She Who Has No Master(s) collective, as a space in which to share our experiences and collaborate creatively. Visibility and community, however, have been slow aspects to form — and I would say much of this is due to racial expectations and biases in U.S. society;

there is still a lot of work to be done, that could be done, to fully hear and see all the nuances of the Vietnamese diasporic experience (which has so very many variances in it, no one story is representative).

VKN: What are some of the racial expectation and biases you experience or notice? Do you feel that your book addresses this?

DS: I think the general American perspective on Vietnam is a convoluted mess of a story, that I can't succinctly sum up. But I might say, in the four decades of my own (American) life, I have grown up in an America that perceives Vietnam predominantly, and first, as a war, or a wound, or a spectacle of media and polarizing rhetoric — as a political conundrum — before it ever perceived Vietnam as a culture and a population of equally human people. The narrative has been dominated by white men, military narrative perspectives, and also by the wounds of how America suffered from the war. In my own experience many Americans did not (do not) exactly understand the history of North and South Vietnam — in short, the nuances of the history and the culture.

VKN: When I was in Florida, a man with grey beard who looked like a short Sean Connery, approached me and said, "I am sorry for what we did to your country." I was stirred by his apologetic gesture and felt deep tenderness for him (as I could not understand why a man could apologize for an entire nation, but I guess one could) and did not feel the depth of genuity and sincerity of his country's words until I met him. Have you had an encounter like this?

DS: I have had encounters like this, yes. Often white veterans wanting to share something of their experience in Vietnam, what they suffered from having to fight in a war they may not have fully believed in, that they feel shame for and much conflict. At one music show I played once in Oklahoma, a man came up to me afterward and told me he had been a Marine in the war, and that he felt my music could provide "healing" for many men like himself. I find these moments and encounters tender, and — case by case — some more genuinely felt than others. In the moment, I am always willing to be present for another person's experience. However, in these exchanges I'm also aware of an underlying current that can trouble me. Because we, as Vietnamese-descended people, also have our own stories to tell and feel our way through...we are not just here to be a catalyst of either healing or reminder of past horrors to these men who experienced an awful war in a place that, though I have no memory of it myself consciously, lives in me in a much different way than it does in those men. In short, I think it is important to recognize that the Vietnamese people and stories exist — and should be given space to be seen/read – independent of the experiences and perspectives of Americans, especially white men. The Vietnamese diaspora (descended out of circumstances of war, but also so much more, including whole lives spent growing up in America) have their own experiences and art to express. They are not just reflections or obstacles against which the white (male) American perspective of the war plays itself out.

VKN: I am moved and I am happy that you are voicing this. I have felt versions of this pigeonholdedness when I am told to write more "ethnically." Do you feel this pressure when you are creating your own work? My experimental writing feels very Vietnamese to me and yet, because I don't include or write in the "ethnic" markers of my reality, readers have not validated my "fluency" in English and my "fluency" in Vietnamese. It is for this reason that I love reading your book as I felt connected to Vietnam from a remote, intimate place that could not date itself back completely or turned its imbued, all encompassing gaze back to guilt-infested "American culture." I like how the lens of perception is pointed towards art, as it is a language that could annihilate all borders and it is in itself transformative. Your book, in both visual and linguistic form, exhibits this imagination without parameters very well. What kind of conversations did you desire from your work?

DS: These are interesting perceptions, too, especially about your own writing. I see the experimental forms as a just as potent (maybe more so) way of addressing, and resisting, some of these racial-stereotypes and pressures/expectations. My experience of your writing has been a sense that you are working on subtle currents, and they are not (to me) definitely western or typically "ethnic" (which is the way western readers might feel more comfortable with experiencing your "Vietnamese-ness") — instead, there is a sense of another way of experiencing time and narrative and interiority…(I am trying to find the right terms as I try to articulate this…)

One of the problems about the American publishing industry's perception (and expectation) of "ethnic" writers, is simply one of a western-centered mindset: they define the "ethnic" experience as being an immigrant one — how that particular group entered America, becomes assimilated, etc etc. For myself, I was seeking, and still am, how to define — and how to really *feel* — what it means to be of Vietnamese descent in a way that, perhaps, reaches beyond war — beyond our relationship to imposing forces i.e. America and external nations. When I would ask even Vietnamese people what it meant to be Vietnamese, I would be told again and again stories about war — thousands of years of war, against the Americans, French, Chinese, etc. The quiet question inside myself kept wondering who we were before war, and if/how that was possible to perhaps meet, or uncover?… Maybe hints of reaching back to matrilineal society or indigenous perspectives are further questions along this thread. Because I feel that the imposition of the war-dominated "self-definition" (to go back to that earlier term) is largely due also to the advent of a patriarchal paradigm.

VKN: I always felt that US involvement in Vietnam was born from the delirium or an infestation of continuing the machination or war or the language for war because it's only narrative the world seems to speak, but doesn't understand. I feel any war, current or past, is a victim of limitation. That it's hard to imagine a world without wars and to imagine a peaceful existence is to imagine death or misguided impracticality or uncertainty. War is certain and peace feels uncertain? This is why despite our familiarity with the language of war embodied in our being as human time and space, it always feel so foreign or alien to us. This is why I was so drawn to experimentalism and I assume this is the reason why you are drawn to it too because we want to create a political, artist, literary dimension that won't promote predictable narratives that reinforce past certainties: cruelty, genocide, rape, and indifference.

DS: Yes – absolutely. (I wish you could be here to converse with the other women writers on this retreat…!) I would agree with that line of thought — war as a *certainty* that thwarts the fear or discomfort of realizing — of accepting — ambiguity, and how these elements are the basis of much violence — which essentially begins with the conceiving of one body as separate (other) than your own. I think that we are living — in this time and in the west — within a consciousness that defines itself via founding acts of division and separation; and yes, peace — union, stasis — is fairly inconceivable within this concept of humanity. But I see experimental forms, that take into deep consideration the shapes and contexts and narrative constructs of things (and these as important choices to make), as one way of refusing to perpetuate those prevailing ideas. It seems that you have made use of experiments in writing for the same underlying reasons.

VKN: I wish I were there too. Why did you give up on filmmaking? What medium do you feel most at home in?

DS: I feel like writing is very much like breathing and thinking for me, so I might say I am a writer first, but also that I'm not interested in being only a writer anymore. Music is the medium I perhaps enjoy the most, though, because I can lose myself in it – into a state of ethos, feeling, simple expression. As I see it, working in hybrid forms — pursuing *literature* through various modes of expression — is my own attempt to develop myself more wholly, as a person, as a perceiver. If I am to talk about separation (which includes the divisions and disconnects within myself) as a problematic, then maybe I should also use my process to try to rectify that within myself. But also — more simply — I love the way that sound/music engages language differently, perhaps more emotionally, than just seeing it on a page. Same with visuals. I think literature, which is essentially the art of storytelling and of sharing experience, can and should engage all the senses, potentially: language, sound, body, etc. As for filmmaking, for me it was a young pursuit and perhaps I wasn't cut out for that 'industry' ultimately; but I still find myself working with video and experimenting with documentary techniques.

VKN: What is your preferred place to visit when you were in Vietnam or in the world? How has travel help you with writing?

DS: The most resonant places in Vietnam for me to visit were the Champa ruins — namely, the Banh It towers near Quy Nhon — and the caves in the Phong Nha National Park area. I am drawn to natural landscapes, and to the textures and elements of the physical world, rocks and water especially.

VKN: I love Quy Nhon, or the travel from Saigon to Quy Nhon. One could view the height of the sea running beneath the road from the bus. Speaking of resonant places, will you tell me more about Ajar? Its editors/translators. How was the connection established? If I remember accurately, Ajar is born and established in Vietnam, yes? Being published there should widen the demographics of your readers, yes? What is your vision for its publication? Readership-wise? Did you want to have a more direct conversation with Vietnam?

DS: Ajar Press is the brainchild of a Vietnamese poet, Nha Thuyen, and an American poet-translator, Kaitlin Rees. They are based in Hanoi. They publish an online journal, as well as a print one, and they publish a series of bilingual poetry books as well, called Fish Eyes. I connected to them when they reached out to DiaCritics (the Vietnamese diasporic arts and culture blog I mention above) and dialogues ensued from there. I was struck by their feminist and experimental — also, their unabashedly playful — aesthetic bent. Kaitlin Rees just received a PEN Translation grant for a book of poetry she is translating of Nha Thuyen's poems, in fact. I think they are doing a wonderful, daring job of inhabiting and exploring the interstices, so to speak, between languages, time periods, and Vietnam and its diasporas in the west… As for publication hopes and readership, I have to admit I am not strategic, and I try simply to trust. Ultimately, I am always searching for connection, and trying to do the most honest work I can make; and then trust/hope for it to find its readers or listeners or viewers. It is meaningful to me that Ajar Press is based in Hanoi, and that my writing will get to appear as a bilingual book. And I hope it will offer something to the readers that happen to find it.

*

VKN: Our conversation is passing through different geographical boundaries. When we started conversing, you were in Corsica and I was in Brooklyn, conducting our conversation in Ana Božičević's apartment. And, now we are in the same coast; you are back in Portland and I am in Vegas. How does it feel? This transition? How was your retreat? Was it fruitful? Did you accomplish what you wish? Would you generate a similar retreat in the United States? Possibly in the West Coast? What will you do in Portland now that you have returned?

DS: Hi again, Vi, and yes our conversation has carried across geographies...

When I last wrote to you I was listening to the birds outside my window in Corsica, and was being greeted each morning by the sunlight and the sea there...I was sharing meals and stories with 8 other women writers, and we were working on our collaborative reading (a prose-poem with 9 voices, translated into French and Vietnamese, so a trilingual effort...) which we performed at the American Library in Paris on May 27th. So it's been a whirlwind of places and people, voices and sites, and then I was back in Portland, just in time to co-host a Portland-based collaborative event (de-canon.com), and then see my son graduate from high school. So, it has been a full and eventful spring so far.

Being back...first, I'll say that the retreat in Corsica was quite healing, and bonding, to spend that much close time with other women writers, to devote our energy to topics and themes related to being of Vietnam, and to have the gift of being in a beautiful location to do so — was all very special. Meanwhile, the politics of America continue, and I returned to a very tense Portland, just following the racist attack on the train (you may've heard, where two men were killed), which felt, to say the least, quite discomfiting. It's hard to fully enjoy retreat and respite periods, knowing that the divides and violences continue here, and that the racial situations of America (and the world) are impossible to escape, really. I try to sight the small work that I can do in this particular community — which for me amounts to advocating for spaces for voices of color to be heard and represented well. Poetry seems a tenuous resistance effort, but since art is important to me, I try to believe it can be so for others too.

As for what is next: I will work on editing the *Somewhere Else* manuscript for Ajar Press, and keep working on other projects as well. I want to mention the She Who Has No Master(s) collective again and our plan, for next year, to enact our project in Vietnam. So our next retreat and reading event will — hopefully — take place in Vietnam. We are beginning to talk to Ajar Press (and others) about potential interactions/ collaborations. (And would love to have you join us too next time, if possible!) So, my main hope is just to keep having dialogues, and crossing borders, and using art (writing, music, seeing, etc) as a vessel to enact and feel and also record these journeys

Powder Puff

Estella Gonzalez

You can't rush this. Nuh uh. That's why you get up at four in the morning even if you don't have to be at work until nine because you never know when you might run into one of your old boyfriends or worse, one of those old skanky metiches from high school like that cha-cha girl Sonya. So take your time. Ignore your parents, especially your mother who bangs on the door like she's gonna crash through it.

"Apurate Mireya!"

Apura nada. Who knows? Today may be the day Principal Díaz will actually ask you out. Take it easy with the foundation and rub it all the way down to your neck. You want to make sure everybody believes the makeup is your natural skin color.

This is the first Monday of the month so you break out the Prescriptives Virtual Youth Foundation in "Smooth Honey." One shake and a little brown slug pushes through the little hole, goes right on your sponge wedge—fresh squeezed and better than that first morning cigarette. And it really blends into your skin. No more pink eraser look. At least nowadays the girls at the counter don't have to pretend that oh yes, you'll glow just like a pink peach cover girl once you buy this 20-dollar jar of beauty sauce.

Of course you use a sponge wedge, not those little cotton balls Mama used. The beige foundation used to drip over them instead of staying on long enough to be wiped over her face. But once she wiped it on, it stayed on, even when it melted down to her neck. Tía Tonia would bring her samples from The Broadway where she worked the Chanel counter and would get un puño de free samples or "promotions," as she used to call them.

Tía was the rich one in your family. She wore pretty black blouses with the two white backward Cs stitched on them. Her skin always looked smooth like condensed milk, not pink and hard like Mama's. And she wore makeup all the time, not just at home or at parties. And her hands were nice and smooth with long nails covered in pearly reds, browns or purples. But her eyes. If she got too close, she'd scare you. She'd line her eyes like Elizabeth Taylor's "Cleopatra" and then draw her eyebrows real high and thin. But Mama and Daddy thought she looked like an artista, a real movie star. Daddy liked Tía Tonia a lot and would always hug or hold her hand and ask Mama why she didn't look "arreglada" like Tía did. Mama would just laugh.

"Una muñeca," Daddy would say looking at Tía up and down like his head was broken.

*

Once you spread the foundation all evenly, put on the powder. Dust it with a big, clean soft brush. Don't use those cheap velour powder puffs like Mama. After a couple of weeks, they always got sticky thick with dirt, oil and old powder. She always threw them away because they were feos and asquerosos. But ever since Lancôme girl told you how a brush can "evenly distribute" the powder across the pores and actually make the pressed powder in the compact last longer than if you used puffs, you buy that five-piece set with the ebony handles for one hundred dollars. And you charge it because it's not pay day yet and even if it was, you still couldn't afford it since your job as registrar at Fourth Street Elementary School doesn't pay jack shit. Still, it's a great deal since you usually pay about forty dollars for the powder anyway but now it'll last you about six months instead of three. It's like a mini-sacrifice but Principal Diaz is worth every cent, every grain of powder, and every hair on that brush. Not like Daddy. Not like Isaac.

One day, while you watched Mama get ready for Tía's party, Daddy walked in, picked up one of those disgusting powder puffs from the little trash can near the toilet.

"Mira," he said pushing it up to your face. "Te pareces como esta cochinada."

You smelled the beer and you knew he'd been drinking in the garage since morning.

"Mira, mira," he said holding your chin hard, poking your pimples and your eyebrows that looked exactly like your Nana's. You didn't say anything. You just bit your cheek real hard so you wouldn't cry.

"No seas grosero Alejandro," Mama said but Daddy kept poking you until Mama said she'd get you to "fix" yourself up.

*

Next you line your eyes with good eyeliner. What will it be today?

Copper Penny by Estēe Lauder or Black Vellura by Borghese? You decide on Copper Penny since it's more of a daytime color than the Vellura. You'll save that one for clubbing with your comadres.

You're careful to follow the lash line below the eye so you don't poke yourself like you did so many times before you got the hang of it. Then you pencil the top lid very slowly, pressing a little harder so there aren't any spaces; you want smooth, solid lines. Mama always used liquid eyeliner. When you started, you used that "Big Red" pencil liner from Maybelline but it got so hard after you first used it, you had to melt it with a match in the girls' bathroom to put it on before class started.

You bought that eyeliner at Thrifty's half a mile from your house. You took a bus there instead of walking to the Kmart on the corner because the guy you had a crush on since junior high was a Jehovah and sold *Atalaya* magazines in front of Thrifty's with his father every Saturday. Isaac and his father would be dressed in suits and ties and they'd stand right near the doors, *Atalayas* pressed to their chests. You'd walk by and say "hi" to him. The first time Isaac didn't look at you. But you knew he was just embarrassed. His father always embarrassed him. One time he made Isaac sit on a kitchen chair in his front yard and practice the accordion. Every kid on the block stopped playing, watching TV, whatever they were doing, and stood right in front of the yard yelling awful things like "You look like a fag Isaac." "Sounds like my grandma's records."

Then this one kid, Paul, a real vago, threw his football at Isaac's face. Isaac dropped the accordion and ran to the door. But it was locked. He kept banging on it but his parents wouldn't open it. His father shouted something from the window. You couldn't hear because of all the kids shouting but as soon as he yelled it, Isaac sat back down and started practicing again. Some of the other kids started throwing rocks but Isaac just kept playing. You ran back into the house, crying like his father had made you sit in the front yard with him. First thing you did was lock the bathroom door and pull out one of the drawers. You looked for the Borghese compact with the little crest. When you found it, you powdered every inch of your face. Pat, pat, pat. You made sure you covered every purple pimple on your face with the stuff. Pat, pat, pat. You felt a little better and left the makeup on until Isaac's parents let him in the house.

*

Don't overdo the eye shadow. Do it light and "playful" like the lady at the counter told you. You don't want to scare the kids at school. And you don't want Principal Díaz to think you're desperate like that piruja Sonya who flirts with any man who'll look at her boobs. She still piles on the cheap makeup an inch thick and wears those V-neck blouses like she did in high school. She still has the biggest boobs you ever saw.

The last time you saw Sonya, it was during Back-To-School registration. You were helping parents out with registering their kindergartners when she walked in. The moment you saw that wild curly hair and those boobs, you knew it was her. But you couldn't believe she had a kid with her. She always used to say she never wanted any mocosos to get in the way of her life. But there she was, standing in line with all the other parents, registering this little girl who looked just like a mini-Sonya.

"Hi Sonya," you said.

Sonya looked at you like she didn't know you. She just nodded her head and started filling out the form you pushed in front of her. You saw the circles under her eyes even if she did try to hide them with concealer. You use concealer too but the good kind: Anti Cernes Quick Cover by Chanel. It's so good you don't even know how to say the first two words.

You remembered the lunch periods in high school when she used to sit with all her cheerleader friends and pull out all those lipstick tubes from her imitation Gucci bag. Sonya's favorite was the gold one with silver, swirly lines. Estēe Lauder of course.

"Hey, check out this color," she'd say, puckering her lips.

"You look like Nastassia 'Kinky,'" one of the other cheerleaders would say.

Then they'd all laugh like a bunch of payasas.

She didn't know it, but sometimes you'd watch her from a bathroom stall to see what color she would put on for the next period. One time she caught you.

"What are you doing you little perve?" she said. "What are you staring at?"

You came out all cool, pretending like you were just there to piss and leave.

"I'll kick your ass next time you do that," she said as you walked out the door.

You did it again, but not until after she got pregnant. By then, she would just splash her face with water, run her hands through her curly hair and run out to class.

That time you registered her kid, Sonya wore makeup but it was that corriente stuff, like Cornsilk or Almay. Cheap cosmetics you could buy at any supermarket. You could tell she didn't rub the foundation around her neck like she should have to make it look natural. And her face looked like it was missing something. You couldn't figure it out until she kissed her little girl. Pues, she wasn't wearing any lipstick! It was funny, because Mama always used to point to her when she walked to school in front of your house and say, "Esa si sabe como pintarse."

And when she walked back home from cheerleading practice, Daddy would be standing out there watering the lawn, watching her walk by. His head would swivel almost all the way around his neck. He wouldn't say it out loud, but you could see his lips say "Que muñeca."

But Isaac, he was the one who really showed you how a girl with good makeup could get whatever she wanted. And whatever she didn't want. By your senior year, he was saying "hi" to you. He even kissed you a couple of times but he never walked you home or took you out to dances. He took Sonya. That year, Sonya got Isaac and his baby.

That was five years ago. Ni modo. There was a reason you were on the other side of the counter and she wasn't. You wanted to ask her if she married Isaac. Or if he left her for another, prettier woman who could make herself up better. Would Isaac have loved you instead? You didn't have the big boobs, but you wouldn't have cheated on him like Sonya did with the D.J. at the Spring Fling dance. Deep down, you hoped he had found out. You hoped he punched Sonya like Daddy punched Mama when she caught him kissing Tía Tonia in their bedroom.

Then Isaac walked into the office. Just like that. He was carrying a little white fuzzy thing in one hand and a cup of coffee. When he got closer to Sonya's little girl, he crouched down. You could only see his thick black hair from the counter but you knew he looked the same.

"You forgot your kitty sweetie," he said. You could feel him smiling. The little girl smiled too and grabbed her kitty and his face. He kissed her. Just like that. Then he got up and kissed Sonya. She smiled like he'd given her a stuffed kitten too.

*

After putting on some blush—Clarin's "Mystique"—you can finally put on the lipstick. Last week you wore the Borghese's "Burnt Sugar," which was a little too shimmery, a little too piruja. How about something a little sensuous, yet delicate today? Dr. Diaz still hasn't really noticed you but he checked out Sonya during registration. Just like Daddy, his head was going up and down, up and down. How about Clinique's "Sugared Toffee"? Put on the Underwear for Lips lip primer first. When Dr. Diaz finally sees the quality makeup you use, he'll forget about Sonya and her powder puff face.

You remember how Isaac, before he dumped you and started going around with Sonya, told you how pretty you looked with lipstick (Avon's Creamy Caramel?). How it made your lips look sexier and how you kept hoping he'd notice and maybe kiss you again because your mother said, "El maquillaje es magia." And she should know because she and Daddy stayed married for 40 years. You never saw her without makeup, ever. You know she slept with it on because when you made the beds in the morning, you found lipstick smeared on her pillow. It's not like she worked in an office or anything. Mama made springs in this hot little factory way out in Long Beach. Every day, especially in the summer, her eye shadow, eyeliner and mascara melted like the water colors you painted at school.

Mama kept little sample compacts hidden away in every single drawer of the house. Whenever you looked for a match or a fork, there was always a mini-compact clattering around the drawer like some old piece of candy. All over the house, you'd find little green, blue, and black compacts with gold lettering. Her favorite was the Borghese because it had this little silver crest.

"A sign of royalty," she'd say. "Para una princesa italiana."

Then she'd pat, pat the powder on her face until her skin looked like the rubber on your pink eraser. You couldn't wear makeup until you were 16 but you stole a compact anyway. Maybe Sonya would finally notice you, invite you over to her special table for lunch.

*

Washing makeup off is another story. Soap and water won't cut it if you don't want eye-shadow and mascara smeared all over your pillowcase. And you know Mama won't put up with it. And you better not say anything about the lipstick on her pillow.

"No seas tan cochina!" she told you after she caught you using the Neutrogena bar and nothing else. "Un regalo," she said after putting down the Lancôme Effacil eye make-up remover in front of you.

You wonder if you'll ever tell her to shove that remover up her ass. Just because you live with her and Daddy, doesn't mean they can still boss you around. After all, you pay them $300 a month in rent and you never bring any men over to your room, not that there are any men to bring around. Pero que verguenza having to tell a future boyfriend, like maybe Dr. Díaz, that he can't go over to your place because your parents won't let you. You can always move out but you're trying to save up to go back to school and rents are so high in L.A. and what about your monthly trips to the Prescriptives counter, not to mention your stops with the consultants at Chanel, Dior, Borhgese, Clarins, Clinique, Estēe Lauder and Lancôme? No, it's just not time yet.

Then that scene with Dr. Diaz. When he stopped by your desk, your heart started thumping fast. Yes, this would be the day your relationship started. What would it be, coffee at the Igriega's Panaderia or a drink at the Red Onion? And he asks you if you can stay late tonight and help with finishing up the registration.

"Of course," you say, your heart like a big, bloody cut because you get to spend a late night with this man more beautiful than the Christmas promotions of all your favorite cosmetic lines.

"Can you help train someone for me?" he asks, his dark red lips growing larger, swallowing you up into their warm softness.

You nod but all you're thinking is Baby, I would die for you. Just like that Prince song. And even when he brings in Sonya to train, you could care less because all you know is that you get to spend more time with this man you decided you love as much as those fresh jars of foundation lining the bottom of your bathroom cabinets.

*

Use one of those round cotton pads, the ones that look like little quilts. They absorb all the dirt and grime from the most cochina faces. Makeup remover can even lighten up the brownest of skin, at least that's what Tía Tonia with her condensed milk skin told you.

So you rub, and rub but you're still as brown as those clay bowls Mama uses to serve pozole for Daddy. One night, while taking a break from the training, after you saw Dr. Díaz trying to kiss Sonya in the supply room, you rub the Effacil so hard into your face you leave little red patches on your skin. Through that door crack you could see them rubbing their faces against each other, like they were animals. Who knows how long you stood there? It was like watching a movie. Before you knew it, they were done and Sonya was rubbing her hair down and pulling out her Estēe Lauder lipstick tube from her back pocket.

"Nastassia Kinky," you whispered.

And they both looked at you through that crack.

"Bitch," Sonya said.

Dr. Diaz put his arms around her and held her. And you? You went back to your desk pulled out the brand new Chanel compact, looked at your face. You kept looking even after Dr. Díaz and Sonya walked out of the supply room. You didn't look at him when he called your name. You just nodded when he asked you to lock the door before you left.

And so you rub and rub but your skin's no lighter, or whiter than it was before. It never will be, no matter how hard you rub, no matter how many times Dad pokes you. No matter what. Punto.

*

Today, no today you can't do it. You can't step into that steaming water. You can't rummage through your jars. You can't even pick out some pinche cotton pad. No, today it just doesn't suena. You just feel like that used up powder puff Daddy shoved into your face that day. You open up your closet. Maybe the jars can work their magia on you just by looking at them. But then you remember that Estēe Lauder lipstick tube bulging through Sonya's back pocket and all you see is liquid skin sitting there, flaking inside glass.

La Llorona at the Saloon

José Angel Araguz

There are no more dances there.
When she clocks in,
the batwings sound

as if they are ready to drop.
She lays the silver down
and watches faces

melt off the backs of spoons.
Then she crosses herself,
clears her throat,

places the moon at the window.
Some nights, a moth
drifts towards it

and rests on the glass.
Moth legs,
directionless,

slowly turn, soothe
the gray face
with its body.

The Chemist's Wife

Em Rose

In the summer that my neighbor's husband got stopped and sent to Rikers, I rode with her on visiting days, since she hated going that trip alone. We made a ladies' day of it twice a month, whenever his last name fell on Saturday, catching two trains out to Queens Plaza and stopping for green chilaquiles and runny fried eggs before catching the 100-Limited through Ditmars and over that long bridge out to the island.

A few times, I noticed the same man on the bus – improbable odds, but he was distinctive-looking: a gap-toothed little man who moved swiftly on aluminum crutches. Sometimes our eyes met, and he had fast-moving eyes just like a ticker tape feed, like he was racking numbers inside, taking stock of us all.

Sometimes I went in through screening with my neighbor to visit Pikachu (what we all called her husband: a corny wisecrack nickname for a round-ish yellow guy) because I loved Pika, too – like an uncle. Before he got locked up, he used to spin me out across their living room dancefloor, since he was the only man for blocks who could really work a salsa, where bachata was king and not my thing so much. But, just as often, I waited outside for her, trying to make myself scarce in the CO staff parking lot. I'd spent enough time on the visiting floor growing up and I knew that she and Pikachu could use the hour to themselves. I settled on a lamppost's concrete base, happy to disappear in a book.

That day I was tucked in the CO lot reading Chekhov stories when the little man on crutches from the bus came right up to me. He eyed me intently and asked if I had a light. I said no problem and asked could I get a square. His energy was sturdy, like somebody who was used to spending a whole lot of time waiting. He smoked Newport 100s, my old brand. I thumbed my light at him, and he looked at my book. I laughed when he said, "nice taste," and he told me "The Bet" was his favorite story.

"You know this?" I asked.

"Yeah, I read all that way back," he said. "I'm Frank," he offered out his hand.

"They call me Venezuela." We shook.

I asked Frank how he got into Chekhov. He said it was a long story. I told him I had time, so, he broke down for me his old hustle. He said:

"There's this place out in Jersey, sells paperbacks wholesale, priced by the yard with the covers torn off. They're meant for recycling, illegal for resale. We used to buy crateloads – similar to how folks do with secondhand clothes by the pound, but that's easier: less cumbersome to run with in a bust, less illegal. Books are trickier. In the nineties, my cousin Chucho and I had a citywide stripped book empire.

"We bought a seafoam Econoline at auction, $700 flat: graffitied-up, rusted, two bolts shy of scrapyard, but she ran, and she was roomy. They don't make them like that these days. None of us had papers, let alone a valid license, and the van was uninsured, too, and needed commercial plates. But we knew a guy in Harlem, got us fake plates, $50.

"We'd always get harassed by cops, but, back then before 9/11, these things seemed a little softer. I'd just tell them I'd left my ID at home, give a fake name and address. Chucho saw my tickets one day – I had just three by then – and they were made out to Juan Pablo Duarte, Ramon Matias Mella, Francisco del Rosario Sanchez. 'Coño, you're a real idiot,' he told me, 'You got all the founding fathers ticketed!'

"Well, we sold most books for $1, some for $2 – the Stephen Kings, the Grishams. We were stacking money fast. We never cared much for a bank account, so we had $30,000 cash in the one-bedroom we shared. We used to fling it around us in the air, like a couple of rich cartoon men. We thought we were going to be millionaires off of our book-selling hustle.

"But Chucho was a mess. He lost thousands gambling or buying girls or cocaine. He was a fool, I'd always tell him. I would have disowned him early on if he wasn't blood family, and, after his fool ass lost our van keys he was the only one who could hotwire it. He had somehow worked out the trick to it – beast predated Watergate – so I had to keep that lunk around.

"One day this girl showed up – woman, I mean – petite, brown, with a nose ring, big eyes. She was a professor of comparative literature at Columbia University. She was stacked, but she dressed classy: red wine lipstick, sexy sweaters. She poked around our table, asked if we had any real books. I said, 'they're all real,' but I dug around for some Shakespeare plays, thinking that could be her thing. She shrugged back at me like, 'oh well.' I was feeling her, got fuddled. I asked what she was looking for and she said she liked the Russians. I promised I had plenty, just not right on me then. I told her to come back soon. When I tell you, I went swimming through those books out in New Jersey picking every Russian name. When she came back, she asked if I knew those books – I didn't. But I lied. I set out straight away to reading all of them: Chekhov, Pushkin, Gogol. I was so nuts to impress her, I made sure to track down any other books she mentioned after that: Fanon, Baraka, Kafka, Marx. Whenever she'd come, I'd leave Chucho the stand and take her for coffee, talk for hours. I was wild for her ."

He paused then, trailing off right there. "What happened?" I asked him.

"I saw her with Chucho one day. I could've killed him right then. And, then, she stopped coming. I had her landline. But she just never picked up.

"Not long after that, we were in the Lincoln Tunnel, morning rush, and the van up and died on us. Chucho set to jimmying all his steering column wiring, but it was taking too long. Car honking, drivers cursing, and the flatbed tow truck rolled right up with an NYPD squad car trailing.

"Well, we took one good look at ourselves: both undocumented, van uninsured, hotwired to start, fake plates, jam-packed loaded with illegal books for resale. There was only one thing to do. I shook Chucho's hand; we split. That was that. He went one way, and I went another, moving fast as my crutches go. We left our van right there in the morning rush hour Lincoln Tunnel. That was the end of our business venture as literature salesmen."

When my neighbor came out and found me, I told Frank "nice to meet you" and said I hoped I'd see him around. I wondered why he was out at Rikers and why he didn't go in, if he was waiting on someone, too, but I didn't think too much of it.

On the bus ride back to Queens Plaza to catch both trains back home, my neighbor was usually silent, older-looking than she was. But, this time, she seemed restless, buzzing, and by Astoria Boulevard she was whispering, excited, talking about could I keep a secret.

Pikachu had told her they were planning to go on strike in a coordinated effort with jails and prisons across the country. I asked how they were organizing. She couldn't tell me but it involved the smuggling in and out of books. The little bit she told me past that, I swore never to share. She grew quiet for a while. She focused out the window. I looked at her lap. When she shifted her weight, her handbag uncovered something that she held, tightly like a Bible, and I realized what it was: a yellowed-up mass market copy of Sun Tzu's *The Art of War* with the front cover of it stripped off.

How to be Courageous: Llanto Mundo

Angie Cruz

On a cold fall evening Rosa Alcalá and Urayoán Noel read from their books at Wordup Bookstore in Washington Heights. Rigoberto González, Sheila Maldonado and I were in the audience. So of course we uncorked a bottle of wine and started a conversation about all things latinidad.

Urayoán Noel: Rosa and Rigoberto, where does your courage come from? I'm thinking about you two because I think you're both so amazing.

Angie Cruz: Are you asking about the courage in the writing?

UN: Even the courage to step out into some spaces that we occupy, right? In some ways, moving in spaces where we're always the marginalized. I see you both, Rosa and Rigoberto, as so fearless—

AC: How do you define fearless?

UN: You know, fierce—

AC: Like in the writing or...?

UN: Yes and in how you carry yourself. You're both people I admire for that. But I know that being an artist is difficult. There's doubt and self-doubt and a lot of struggle. There's a lot of isolation. There's a lot of mental illness. Anxiety. So how do you manage that? There's also an expectation that you can't be weak, you can't be vulnerable, you can't struggle.

Rigoberto González: How do we stay put together when we really aren't? I think that's a big misconception. I was thinking about this earlier. I told you about the young man at the National Book Awards. It was Danez Smith. This fierce poet. I said, Danez, you know you look amazing in that blue suit! And he says, oh yea, you know I wanted to be a young you. And I was just like, what?! But I know what he meant though. Because, think about it. As a queer writer, so many of my queer mentors are dead, right? And also in the latino community, they burn out so quickly. So those elders are no longer around. There's so few—They're just burnt out. They're not publishing, they're not making public appearances anymore, they're completely outside of the—

AC: …but is it that they're not writing or is it that they're not being invited for public appearances or solicited? I think there are some writers who are struggling with or not wanting to participate in digital media, etc and that may make them less visible. I mean, you'd mention Danez Smith who I think is wonderful at social media and in it he appears to be confident and thriving, but then I saw this Facebook update by him, saying that he had had a difficult year and I wondered if he could only admit to it now that he was nominated for a National Book Award, etc. So it makes me think about vulnerability. When and how we admit to our vulnerability to a larger audience. But yes, I have noticed some writers who just don't know or don't have the energy to navigate this contemporary digital moment, and sometimes even, they start to feel irrelevant because of it.

RG: I mean, I feel that sometimes, because, we're digital immigrants. We're not digital natives. This generation of writers is moving through the space in a very different way. I tell my classes that I think I'm going to reach retirement much sooner than I thought I would. Also, I begin to understand the people that came before me. Because they're like, you know, you get tired. You get tired and you really want to claim that space that you're not allowed to claim. We were having that conversation earlier about the expectations on us. Because of who we are and what we do and can do, and everybody wants a piece of us. The industry, our students, our colleagues. And we give up so much. So there comes a time when you just want to spend time to yourself, and the only way to do that is to really cut yourself off completely. Because it's an all or nothing, zero-sum game in so many ways.

AC: I just spent some time with Sandra Cisneros in Pittsburgh. And Sandra was talking about activist burnout, although I don't think she called it that. She was saying how she once had this feeling or need to rescue everyone. Maybe guilt of being working class, or being one of the few. And how she just gave and gave and she felt like it was never enough, people wanted more. It sometimes feels to me like we cannot fill the well of need, right? And then she told me about Ursula LeGuin who said, I'm going to sanctuary. And everyone's like, what's the sanctuary? It's a reclaiming of space, a space to drop out and recharge.

So I asked Sandra, but what if we stop doing the work then who the hell's going to do it? There aren't that many latinas out there that have her power and visibility. She's like, I passed the baton. And I said, to who?! And I wonder, is that what you mean by retirement? Where you say, you know what, I did my work. I pass on the baton.

RG: I think so. And you have to trust that the world's not going to collapse. And first thing to admit is that you're not the one holding it up. But it takes a big moment to get there because the whole time you think you are. And that's why you don't give up. And that's why you keep doing. And that's why, for so many of us, the world does collapse on top of us before we hand it over to somebody else. What do you think?

Rosa Alcalá: You said something earlier, that we don't have to hold it all together. And I think that sometimes the appearance of having it all together is part of the burden. I started late. I got my first book published at 40. My first manuscript, the one I wrote in my MFA, it got rejected and rejected. I didn't know that part of it wasn't just writing good poems. Maybe that manuscript was not worth publishing, period, but I didn't have the support and the network to do the things that I needed to do for my work. I just thought the work would speak for itself. Like if I was good enough, I would be recognized eventually.

AC: And what do you mean by recognition? What is the expectation of recognition? Is it a literary award?

RA: I'm not even talking about awards. Because that's really not my world. I'm talking about getting published initially. I'm talking about even getting a book out. Because my work didn't fit in neatly anywhere. I think all of those categories have opened up, have shifted, and become more porous, but suddenly I was meeting people who were exploring, even if the form in which they were doing it was different, similar issues about identity, for example. In an experimental way or whatever. I think my work is very straightforwardly lyric, but people call it this other thing. Whatever. But I feel like there's more space for me.

Sheila Maldonado: I put you in the New York School. Because Brainard shows up so much. I wanted to teach you, but I didn't know what school, but I feel the conversational…

RA: Yeah. But there's a problem with lineage. Like you should or could only claim certain people. My work takes from all over the place. I think we build our own literary lineage—

SM: Right, but it was cool to teach schools and movements but then you're like, this is kind of all bullshit. But it's a good place to start. Like I taught Nuyorican and New York School and Black Arts and Central American Poetry. Like that's not a school— ::laughter::

RA: Actually, in those *You* poems that I read tonight, a lot of them take place in my twenties, these vignettes. One of the things I should write about is leaving my temp job and going to the Nuyorican Poets' Cafe. Because at the time I was going to St. Marks Poetry Project and also the Nuyorican. Those were influences. They were both performance spaces but [with] different kinds of performances.

SM: Same.

RA: in some ways there was a fluidity in those spaces that wasn't acknowledged in the literary world and in publishing.

UN: You mean in the 90s, right?

RA: Yeah. There was a fluidity in those spaces. Not so much—

SM: Everybody knows each other. Like if you're downtown, everybody knows each other.

RA: But I didn't see that reflected in the books.

SM: In school, in academia. That's where it's not reflected.

RA: Right. And then you have to choose, you are this or you are that. It wasn't that you were being asked directly to choose, but it's like, how do we place you? So, for a long time I thought, well at some point my work is going to be good enough for someone to publish. And I realized that the times had to change. My work was always sort of doing the same thing. And it's gone through different stages, but I feel like those initial concerns are the same. I looked up a journal that I wrote when I was at Brown doing my MFA in Creative Writing and I was concerned with the very same things that I'm concerned with now. I did not become experimental because I went to Buffalo, you know what I mean? I was still playing with language and form because, I don't know, when you grow up the daughter of an immigrant it's kind of an experimental experience. Your thinking about language a kind of material thing. Writers deal with that relationship to language in different ways but for someone who grew up bilingual–there's so many examples of writers who come from a bilingual background who approach that in a different way–we're all very aware of the materiality of language because we're always outside either English or Spanish. We're always mediating between the two. So for me it wasn't even about winning awards. It was about where is there a place for my work? It took until I was forty but I met some really amazing people who helped me understand that there was a place. Roberto Tejada for one, who is a really important person for me. And then there was Mónica de la Torre, there was Urayoan Noel and Carmen Gimenez Smith. Edwin Torres started at the Nuyorican. Suddenly it's like, there is this community and it's not homogenous.

We're all writing differently.

So going back to the question of vulnerability,—I think some of my students think, you never got a poem rejected! No one ever trashed your poem in workshop. I'm like, honey, you just don't know. I've been through all the rejection and heartache in the world with my writing. I'm in a good spot now. I mean, I'm not famous, but I'm in a good spot. That took a lot of work. They need to see it. I think that vulnerability is part of our mentorship. It isn't about just being a perfect, it's about showing the difficulty. Some of our students are parents. They're not getting a lot of money to go to school. They're struggling financially. As I'm getting older, I feel more okay with being vulnerable. I think it's scarier when you're a young woman. Because we know what happens to young women who are vulnerable or show vulnerability. But as I'm getting older I feel like, that's okay. I can even show my maternal side. I'm much more comfortable as I'm getting older and it's nice to feel that both my writing is okay just the way it is and—I mean I always want to be better, but I always wanted to write like other people, but I feel like I've come to accept it. That's why CantoMundo was such a beautiful experience, you know? We were there together. But I wish that I had had a place like that to just be. And to talk and get guidance. I almost felt like I was a fellow at CantoMundo. I felt like my soul was being fed.

AC: Being that all of you have participated in CantoMundo as either faculty or fellows, what has happened for all of you, that's different, in that context, that has not happened in other workshops? What is possible in that kind of space like CantoMundo that might not be able to happen in another context?

RG: I think all the masks just—

SM: Drop. Yeah, that's true. Well I kept one or two up but—

RG: Well me too but even then, so much so, almost like too many!

AC: What is one of the masks that fell off?

RG: The fear. The fear of showing emotion. In workshop, even if you bring in a poem that's very personal, you just have to be rigid. But I think that in this space people allow themselves to cry. They allow themselves to have these vulnerable emotions. But let me tell you: it was overwhelming. I was shocked the first night. I went back to my hotel room and I was like, I don't know if I can handle this another day!

SM: What that made me think of was, when I went to Brown. I was 17. I did my undergrad there. They had this thing called TWTP, which is Third World Transition Program. CantoMundo sometimes reminded me of that which scared the shit out of me, because a lot of things came out. This time though I'm older and now I'm the facilitator in some way even though I'm not faculty. Everyone's super young like 20s, 30s. It's a real difference in ages.

AC: Is it because that's who applies mostly?

SM: They're mostly in MFA programs, which is an issue.

UN: I said that in my blog. CantoMundo hasn't decided if it wants to be a feeding ground for MFA-land, or this other thing and it's kind of uneasily doing both—

SM: But I broke down this time. The first time I was like, pull it together. And this time I came in and I called it LlantoMundo… ::laughter::

AC: How do you think it can help produce better work?

SM: It makes you think about a world where you're not isolated.

AC: But does your work change? Like the actual work?

RA: I had a different experience. I was impressed by the diversity of ages. It was impressive, just the diversity as a whole. To have that diversity even within that frame of Latinidad, in age and the kind of work that was being represented, and the different backgrounds. All of that I thought was really good to see. Just the aesthetic approaches were—

SM: Super varied. Yeah.

RA: And I felt an openness that I don't always feel. Like an openness to whatever I wanted to give them in workshop. This willingness and eagerness. I think the space was created for that possibility. I left there feeling like I got something that I needed. I know everyone saw us there as the people that were going to teach them something, and I know it sounds corny but I really did leave there feeling like I—

SM: like you were taught.

RA: Yeah. Like I was taught.

AC: But how does it change your work?

RA: You're like, enough of the feely-feelies!

SM: It makes you more of an activist. It makes you more aware of everybody. You want to have everyone know who you met. I wanted everybody to know who I met. I was like, I didn't know these people existed. You just kind of wanted—

UN: Didn't that make you angry? Because that made me vulnerable, all the crying. You and I always joke around. You see also people that you know in a very vulnerable space, but also it made me angry because I thought even in New York, you're in this bubble and being Latino is kind of a secondary identification. Boricua or Dominican. You have the privilege of secondary identification. And when you're in that space you see this shit matters. And Latinos always have an epistemological identity crisis. No one knows what it means and it erases blackness, Latinos can be white or whatever, so there's this epistemological uncertainty about what it means and then you go into here and realize this shit matters. This is really urgent and—

AC: ...the work itself feels urgent.

RG: The people coming together it makes it me feel like at least when you're in New York, you can opt out of it

AC: Does it almost feel like the work is being heard,finally? Like in a different way?

RG: Like by your audience. We all say, well who's your audience? And there we're like, well this is our audience! We don't have to explain Spanish, cultural—

AC: There's not all the translation.

RA: I teach in a bilingual MFA program and I've been thinking a lot about, what role do I play in academia? What do I make possible? And I think CantoMundo had me return to my day job thinking it is so important what we do. All of this stuff is written about how horrible the MFA system is, and it has problems, I agree. But if I hadn't gotten an MFA at Brown I wouldn't be where I am now. It opened up worlds that I wouldn't have had access to. I still had to struggle after that because I didn't have all those connections, I didn't know how to do what I needed to do to become a writer, and I continued to work temp jobs and waitress after that, but let me tell you: Brown was the first time I left left New Jersey. So I see MFA programs as opportunities for certain students to maybe be able to discover something beyond. It gave me something that I wouldn't have found on my own. I can work to better that system of the MFA and TAships and all this stuff, but it reminded me that there are students in our program like me that I can say, oh you should send here, you should be doing this, and they wouldn't have gotten it any other way unless they had been in the program. Maybe there should be more spaces besides an MFA for that to happen..

AC: ...like CantoMundo.

RA: Right. But I don't see the MFA program as this completely evil sort of thing.

AC: Thank you for the conversation.

Tal'-s-Go Gal'-Quo-Gi Di-Ded'-Qua-S-Do-Di Tsa-La-Gi Di-Go-Whe-Li / Beginning Cherokee

Qwo-Li Driskill

I-gv-yi-i Tsa-la-gi Go-whe-lv-i: A-sgo-hni-ho-'i / First Cherokee Lesson: Mourning

Find a flint blade
Use your teeth as a whetstone

Cut your hair
Talk to shadows and crows

Cry your red throat raw

Learn to translate the words you miss most:
dust *love* *poetry*

Learn to say *home*

My cracked earth lips
drip words not sung
as lullabies to my infant ears
not laughed over dinner
or choked on in despair
No

They played dead until
the soldiers passed
covered the fields like corpses
and escaped into the mountains
When it's safe we'll find you
they promised
But we were already gone
before sunrise

I crawl through a field of
twisted bodies to find them
I do everything *Beginning Cherokee*
tells me
Train my tongue
to lie still
Keep teeth tight
against lips
Listen to instruction tapes
Study flash cards

How can I greet my ancestors in a language they don't understand

My tear ducts fill with milk
because what I most love
was lost at birth

My blood roars skin to blisters
weeps haunted calls of owls
bones splinter
jut through skin

until all of me
is wounded
as this tongue

Ta-li-ne-i Tsa-la-gi Go-whe-lv-i: A-ni-s-gi-li / Second Cherokee Lesson: Ghosts

Leave your hair
at the foot of your bed

Scratch your tongue
with a cricket's claw to speak again

Stop the blood with cornmeal

Your ancestors will surround you as you sleep
keep away ghosts of generals presidents priests
who hunger for your
rare and tender tongue

They will keep away ghosts
so you have strength
to battle the living

Stories float through lives
with an owl's sudden swooping
I knew some Cherokee
when I was little
My cousins taught me
My mother watches it all happen again
sees ghosts rush at our throats

with talons drawn like bayonets
When I came home speaking
your grandmother told me
I forbid you to speak that language
in my house
Learn something useful

We sit at the kitchen table
As she drinks iced tea
in the middle of winter
I teach her to say *u-ga-lo-ga-go-tlv-tv-nv*/ tea
across plastic buckets of generic peanut butter
wonder bread diet coke
Try to teach her something useful

I am haunted by loss
My stomach is a knot of serpents
and my hair grows out
as owl feathers

Tso-i-ne-i Tsa-la-gi Go-whe-lv-i: A-nv-da-di-s-di / Third Cherokee Lesson: Memory

Raid archeologists' camps
and steal shovels
to rebury the dead

Gather stories like harvest
and sing honor songs
Save the seeds
to carry you through the winter

Bury them deep in your flesh

Weep into your palms
until stories take root
in your bones
split skin
blossom

There are stories caught
in my mother's hair
I can't bear the weight of

Could you give me a braid
straight down the middle
of my back just the way I like
So I part her black-going-silver hair
into three strands
thick as our history
radiant as crow wings

This is what it means to be Indian
Begging for stories in a living room
stacked high with newspapers magazines baby toys

Mama story me

She remembers
Great Grandmother Nancy Harmon
    who heard white women
    call her uppity Indian during

a quilting bee
and climbed down their chimney with
a knife between her teeth

She remembers
flour sack dresses
tar paper shacks
dust storms blood escape

She carries fire on her back
My fingers work swiftly as spiders
and the words that beat in my throat
are dragonflies

She passes stories down to me
I pass words up to her
Braid her hair

It's what she doesn't say
that could destroy me
what she can't say
She weeps milk

Nv-gi-ne-i Tsa-la-gi Go-whe-lv-i: U-de-nv / Fourth Cherokee Lesson: Birth

Gather riverbank clay
to make a bowl

Fill it with hot tears

Strap it to your back
with spider silk

Keep your flint knife close
to ward off death
and slice through umbilical cords

Be prepared for blood

Born without a womb
I wait for the crown of fire
the point where further stretching is impossible
This birth could split me
I nudge each syllable into movement
Memorize their smells
Listen to their strange sleepy sounds
They shriek with hunger and loss
I hold them to my chest and weep milk
My breasts are filled with tears

I wrap my hair around their small bodies
a river of owl feathers

See they whisper *We found you*
We made a promise

    This time we'll be more careful
Not lose each other in
the chaos of slaughter

We are together at sunrise

from dust we sprout love and poetry
We are home
Greeting our ancestors
with rare and tender tongues

Contributors

Isabel Acevedo is a Puerto Rican poet now residing in Milledgeville, Georgia where she is pursuing her MFA in poetry. Her work has appeared or is forthcoming in the *Santa Ana River Review*, *Berkeley Poetry Review*, and *Tule Review*. She also serves as Assistant Poetry Editor of *Arts & Letters*.

Rosa Alcalá is the author of three poetry collections, most recently *MyOTHER TONGUE*. Her poems are included in *American Poets in the 21st Century: Poetics of Social Engagement* (eds., Claudia Rankine and Michael Dowdy), among other anthologies. The recipient of an NEA Translation Fellowship and a finalist for a PEN Translation Award, she is the editor and co-translator of *Cecilia Vicuña: New & Selected Poems* (Kelsey Street Press, forthcoming). She teaches in the University of Texas at El Paso's Bilingual MFA Program.

A CantoMundo fellow, **José Angel Araguz** has had poems recently in *Huizache* and *Salamander*. He is a Ph.D. candidate in Creative Writing and Literature at the University of Cincinnati. Author of six chapbooks and the collection *Everything We Think We Hear*, he runs the poetry blog *The Friday Influence*.

Firelei Báez was born in Santiago de los Caballeros and lives and works in New York. She makes intricate works on paper and canvas that are intrinsically indebted to a rigorous studio practice as well as large scale sculpture. Through a convergence of interest in anthropology, science fiction, black female subjectivity and women's work; her art explores the humor and fantasy involved in self-making within diasporic societies, which have an ability to live with cultural ambiguities and use them to build psychological and even metaphysical defenses against cultural invasions. Báez received an M.F.A. from Hunter College and a B.F.A. from The Cooper Union's School of Art and studied at The Skowhegan School of Painting and Sculpture. She has had solo exhibitions at the Utah Museum of Contemporary Art and at Pérez Art Museum Miami. In 2016 and 2017 she will participate in group and solo museum exhibitions including *Vessel of Genealogies*, Tarble Arts Center, Eastern Illinois University, Chareston, Illinois, *Africa Forecast: Fashioning Contemporary Life*, Spelman College Museum of Fine Art, Atlanta, Georgia, and *Firelei Báez: Bloodlines* at The Warhol Museum, Pittsburgh.

Jeanne Bonner is a writer and journalist based in Connecticut. She is the 2018 winner of the PEN Grant for the English Translation of Italian Literature, given by PEN America. Her essays have been published by *The New York Times*, *CNN Travel* and Catapult. She studied Italian literature at Wesleyan University and has an MFA in Creative Writing from Bennington College.

Amy Sara Carroll is the author of two collections of poetry *SECESSION* (Hyperbole Books, an imprint of SDSU Press, 2012) and *FANNIE + FREDDIE/The Sentimentality of Post-9/11 Pornography* (Fordham UP, 2013), chosen by Claudia Rankine for the 2012 Poets Out Loud Prize. Since 2008, she has been a member of Electronic Disturbance Theater 2.0/b.a.n.g. lab, coproducing the Transborder Immigrant Tool, which was included in the 2010 California Biennial. With EDT 2.0/b.a.n.g. lab and the University of Michigan interdisciplinary workshop the Border Collective, she collaboratively authored *[({ })] The Desert Survival Series/ La serie de sobrevivencia del desierto* (The Office of Net Assessment/ University of Michigan Digital Environments Cluster Publishing Series, 2014), that digitally has been redistributed by CTheory Books (2015), the Electronic Literature Collection, Vol. 3 (2016), CONACULTA E-Literatura/Centro de Cultura Digital (2016), and HemiPress (2017). In 2015, Carroll served as the University of Mississippi Summer Poet in Residence. Summer 2010 and every summer thereafter, she has participated in Mexico City's alternative arts space SOMA. Carroll's critical monograph *REMEX: Toward an Art History of the NAFTA Era* is forthcoming from the University of Texas Press under the auspices of their Mellon Latin American and Caribbean Arts and Cultures Publishing Initiative. Currently, she is a 2017-2018 Society Fellow in Cornell University's Society for the Humanities.

Angie Cruz is the author of *Soledad* and *Let It Rain Coffee*. She has a forthcoming novel, *Dominicana* with Flatiron, NY.

Cherokee poet, scholar, and activist **Qwo-Li Driskill** was raised in rural Colorado. Driskill earned a PhD from Michigan State University. Driskill's poetry engages themes of inheritance and healing, and is rooted in personal Cherokee Two-Spirit, queer, and mixed-race experience. *Walking with Ghosts* (2005), Driskill's first poetry collection, was named Book of the Month by Sable: The LitMag for New Writing and was nominated for the Griffin Poetry Prize. Driskill co-edited, with Colin Kennedy Donovan, *Scars Tell Stories: A Queer and Trans (Dis)ability Zine* (2007), and has work featured in several anthologies, including *Beyond Masculinity: Essays by Queer Men on Gender and Politics* (2008, edited by Trevor Hoppe) and *Speak to Me Words: Essays on Contemporary*

American Indian Poetry (2003, edited by Janice Gould and Dean Rader). The poet is the founder of Dragonfly Rising Press.

Patricia Engel is the author of *The Veins of the Ocean*, *It's Not Love, It's Just Paris*, and *Vida*. She is currently teaching at the University of Miami.

Stephanie Elizondo Griest is the author of four books, including *Around the Bloc: My Life in Moscow, Beijing, and Havana*; *Mexican Enough*; and *All the Agents and Saints: Dispatches from the U.S. Borderlands*. She is Associate Professor of Creative Nonfiction at UNC-Chapel Hill.

F. Marzia Esposito is the author of the novel, "La forma minima della felicità," which was published by Baldini & Castoldi in 2015. She lives in Milan where she teaches dance. She studied film at the Catholic University of Milan. Her short stories have appeared in *Granta*, *GQ*, and other publications.

Sujatha Fernandes is the author of several books, including a memoir about global hip hop, *Close to the Edge* (Verso, 2011) and the forthcoming *Curated Stories: The Uses and Misuses of Storytelling* (Oxford, 2017). Her stories and essays have appeared in the *New York Times*, *The Nation*, *American Prospect*, and a Harper Collins anthology, among other places. Sujatha is a sociology professor at the University of Sydney and the City University of New York. She is an editorial board member of *Transition* magazine. Sujatha is currently working on a book of interlinked short stories entitled *Shadow People*. She tweets at @SujathaTF.

Rina Garcia Chua is affiliated with the Interdisciplinary Studies Department at the University of British Columbia Okanagan. She edited the first anthology of Philippine ecopoetry, *Sustaining the*

Archipelago, published by the University of Santo Tomas Publishing House, and is also the author of several ecocritical essays, short stories, poems, and educational textbooks. Nowadays, she enjoys hiking in the woods of British Columbia as much as she relishes swimming in the warmer corridors of the Pacific Ocean. She also wants to try ice climbing next winter.

Amina Gautier is the author of three short story collections: *At-Risk*, *Now We Will Be Happy* and *The Loss of All Lost Things*. *At-Risk* was awarded the Flannery O'Connor Award, The First Horizon Award, and the Eric Hoffer Legacy Fiction Award. *Now We Will Be Happy* was awarded the Prairie Schooner Book Prize in Fiction, the International Latino Book Award, the Florida Authors and Publishers Association President's Book Award, a National Silver Medal IPPY Award and was a Finalist for the William Saroyan Prize. Her newest collection *The Loss of All Lost Things* was awarded the Elixir Prize in Fiction, The Chicago Public Library Foundation's 21st Century Award, the Royal Palm Literary Award, the Florida Authors and Publishers Association President's Book Award, was a Finalist for the Paterson Prize, and is a Finalist for an IndieFab Award. Ninety-five of Gautier's stories have been published, appearing in *Agni*, *Best African American Fiction*, *Callaloo*, *Glimmer Train*, *Iowa Review*, *Kenyon Review*, *New Stories from the South*, *Prairie Schooner*, *Southern Review*, and *StoryQuarterly* among other places. Her fiction has been supported with fellowships, residencies, and scholarships from the Breadloaf Writer's Conference, Callaloo, The Camargo Foundatio, the Château de Lavigny, Dora Maar, Disquiet International, Hawthornden International Retreat for Writers; Hurston/Wright Foundation, Kimbilio, MacDowell Colony, the Ragdale Foundation, Sewanee Writer's Conference, Ucross Foundation, and Vermont Studio Center.

Estella Gonzalez was born and raised in East Los Angeles, which inspires most of her writing. Her work has appeared in *Puerto del Sol* and *Huizache* and has been anthologized in *Latinos in Lotusland: An Anthology of Contemporary Southern California Literature* published by Bilingual Press. She received a "Special Mention" in *The Pushcart Prize XXXVIII: Best of the Small Presses 2014 Edition* and was selected a "Reading Notable" for *The Best American Non-Required Reading 2011*. Currently, she serves as a contributing editor for Kweli Journal.

Rigoberto González is the author of 20 books of prose and poetry, most recently the book of poetry criticism, *Pivotal Voices, Era of Transition: Toward a 20th Century Poetics*. His awards include the Guggenheim fellowship, NEA, American Book Award, and the USA Rolon fellowship. He's professor of English at Rutgers-Newark, the State University of New Jersey and on the board of trustees of the Association of Writers and Writing Programs (AWP).

Leslieann Hobayan is a poet-writer, yogi, and a member of VONA, a community dedicated to writers of color. Nominated for a Pushcart, her work has appeared or is forthcoming in *The Rumpus*, *Rigorous*, *Barely South Review*, *Generations Literary Journal*, *The New York Quarterly*, *Phati'tude*, *Babaylan: An Anthology of Filipina and Filipina-American Writers*, and *Pinoy Poetics*. She has been awarded the James Merrill Fellowship for Poetry at the Vermont Studio Center, a Mid-Atlantic Arts Foundation writing fellowship for a residency at Millay Colony for the Arts, and an artist grant for the Bread Loaf Orion Environmental Writers Conference. Currently teaching at Rutgers University, she has served as a writing mentor for youth at Urban Word NYC and has taught creative writing at UC-Santa Cruz and Montclair State University. She is at work on a collection of poems as well as a collection of essays.

Marissa Johnson-Valenzuela has published in multiple genres and is the founder of Thread Makes Blanket press. She currently teaches at Community College of Philadelphia.

Rosamond S. King is a creative and critical writer, performer, and artist whose work is deeply informed by her cultures and communities, by history, and by a sense of play. Her poetry has appeared in more than two dozen journals and anthologies, and her manuscript *Rock|Salt|Stone* is forthcoming from Nightboat Books. King has performed in Africa, the Caribbean, Europe, and throughout North America. She is an Associate Professor at Brooklyn College and author of the award-winning scholarly book *Island Bodies: Transgressive Sexualities in the Caribbean Imagination*. Her goal is to make people feel, wonder, and think, in that order.

Sheila Maldonado is the author of the poetry collection *one-bedroom solo* (Fly by Night Press, 2011). Her 2nd publication, *that's what you get*, is forthcoming from Brooklyn Arts Press. Her poems have appeared in *Gulf Coast*, *Ping Pong*, and *The Wandering Song: Central American Writing in the United States*. She is a CantoMundo Fellow and a Creative Capital awardee as part of desveladas, a visual writing collective. She teaches creative writing for The City University of New York.

Carley Moore is an essayist, novelist, and poet. Her debut collection of essays, *16 Pills*, was published in May of 2018 by Tinderbox Editions. Her debut novel, *The Not Wives*, is forthcoming from the Feminist Press in the fall of 2019. In 2017, she published her first poetry chapbook, *Portal Poem* (Dancing Girl Press) and in 2012, she published a young adult novel, *The Stalker Chronicles* (Farrar, Straus, and Giroux). She lives in New York City and teaches at NYU and Bard College.

Vi Khi Nao was born in Long Khánh, Vietnam. She is the author of *Sheep Machine* (Black Sun Lit, 2018), *Umbilical Hospital* (1913 Press, 2017), *A Brief Alphabet of Torture*, which won FC2's Ronald Sukenick Innovative Fiction Prize in 2016, the novel *Fish in Exile* (Coffee House Press, 2016), and the poetry collection *The Old Philosopher*, which won the Nightboat Books Prize for Poetry in 2014. She holds an MFA in fiction from Brown University, where she received the John Hawkes and Feldman Prizes in fiction and the Kim Ann Arstark Memorial Award in poetry.

Urayoán Noel is the author of several books, most recently the critical study *In Visible Movement: Nuyorican Poetry from the Sixties to Slam* (Iowa), winner of the LASA Latino Studies Book Prize, and the poetry collection *Buzzing Hemisphere/Rumor Hemisférico* (Arizona). His bilingual edition of Pablo de Rokha's poetry, *Architecture of Dispersed Life*, is forthcoming with Shearsman Books. Noel is an associate professor of English and Spanish at New York University and also teaches at Stetson University's MFA of the Americas.

Isobel O'Hare is a poet and essayist who has dual Irish and American citizenship. She is the author of the chapbooks *Wild Materials* (Zoo Cake Press, 2015), *The Garden Inside Her* (Ladybox Books, 2016), and *Heartbreak Machinery* (forthcoming from dancing girl press in 2018). Two of her poems appeared in *A Shadow Map: An Anthology by Survivors of Sexual Assault*, published in 2017 by Civil Coping Mechanisms Press. A collaboration with the poet Sarah Lyn Rogers will be published in *They Said: A Multi-Genre Anthology of Contemporary Collaborative Writing*, forthcoming from Black Lawrence Press. Her debut full-length, a collection of erasures of public statements by celebrities accused of sexual abuse, *All This Can Be Yours*, is forthcoming from University of Hell Press.

Ola Osifo Osaze is a trans masculine queer of Edo and Yoruba descent, who was born in Port Harcourt, Delta State and now resides in Houston, Texas. Ola has been a community activist for many years including co-founding the Black LGBTQ+ Migrant Project, working with Transgender Law Center in Oakland, the Audre Lorde Project, Uhuru Wazobia, Queers for Economic Justice and Sylvia Rivera Law Project. Ola is a 2015 Voices of Our Nation Arts workshop (VONA) fellow, and has writings published in *Saraba Magazine*, *Apogee*, *Qzine*, *Black Looks* and the anthologies *Queer African Reader* and *Queer Africa II*. Ola writes to visibilize the myriad journeys and resiliency of queer/trans African migrants, particularly those straddling the worlds of West Africa and North America, and is working on a short story collection that does just that.

Nelly Rosario is author of *Song of the Water Saints*, currently writer/researcher for the MIT Black History Project and the 2017–18 W. Ford Schumann Distinguished Visiting Professor in Democratic Studies at Williams College.

Adriana E. Ramírez is a Mexican-Colombian writer, critic and performance poet based in Pittsburgh. She won the inaugural PEN/Fusion Emerging Writers Prize in 2015 for her novella-length work of nonfiction, *Dead Boys* (Little A, 2016). Her first full-length work of nonfiction, *The Violence*, is forthcoming from Scribner.

Em Rose is an MFA student at CUNY – City College. She holds a B.A. from Columbia, where her poems appeared in student publications *Surgam*, *Quarto*, *Proxy*, and *Fawlt Mag*. She was a Fulbright Fellow in Venezuela, researching maroon history. She previously worked as a housing organizer in Harlem and at GOLES on the Lower East

Side, where she still works as a grant writer. She's received scholarships from the Bread Loaf Translators' Conference and the Squaw Valley Community of Writers. "The Chemist's Wife" is her first published story.

Mahwash Shoaib is a poet, translator and scholar. Her nonfiction, fiction, poetry and scholarly articles have appeared in many anthologies and journals. Her translations of the poetry of Kishwar Naheed, *Wrapped in Dread and Dynamite*, will be published by Upset Press. She currently teaches in Charlotte, North Carolina.

Dao Strom is the author/musician of two books of fiction and the hybrid-forms memoir *We Were Meant To Be a Gentle People* + music album *East/West*. Her bilingual poetry book, *You Will Always Be Someone From Somewhere Else*, will be published by the Hanoi-based Ajar Press in 2018. Her work has received support from RACC, National Endowment for the Arts, Precipice Fund, and the Creative Capital Foundation. She is the editor of diaCRITICS and co-founder of two collective art projects, *She Who Has No Master(s)* and *De-Canon*. www.daostrom.com

Michelle Yasmine Valladares is an immigrant born in India and raised in Kuwait. She is a poet and filmmaker and is the Director of the MFA Program in Creative Writing at City College of New York in Harlem. Her first book is **Nortada, The North Wind**. Her poems have been widely published and she has been nominated for a Pushcart Prize. She won the Distinguished Documentary Achievement from the Independent Documentary Association for "El Diablo Nunca Duerme" co-produced with Lourdes Portillo and Best Latin American Film at Sundance Festival for "O Sertão das Memórias " co-produced with José Araújo.

Acknowledgments

"A Conversation" is adapted from a panel that occurred at the AWP Conference in Tampa, FL on MARCH 8, 2018 celebrating the five-year anniversary of *Aster(ix) Journal.*

"Two Poems" by Leslieann Hobayan first appeared in *Aster(ix) Journal* on MAY 8, 2018.

"Once More, with Feelings" by Mahwash Shoaib first appeared in *Aster(ix) Journal* on OCTOBER 14, 2018.

"Autumn Lessons" by F. Marzia Esposito, translated by Jeanne Bonner first appeared in *Aster(ix) Journal* on OCTOBER 15, 2018. "Esercizi D'Autunno" by F. Marzia Esposito was originally published in *Granta Italia.*

"My Big Gay Essay" by Carley Moore first appeared in *Aster(ix) Journal* on JUNE 9, 2018.

"What is the Difference between Globalization and Neoliberalism?" by Amy Sara Carroll first appeared in *Aster(ix) Journal* on OCTOBER 28, 2013.

"Two Poems" by Rosamond S. King first appeared in *Aster(ix) Journal* on JANUARY 9, 2017.

"Firelei Báez on Generosity and Freedom in Art" by Angie Cruz first appeared in *Aster(ix) Journal* on JULY 6, 2017.

"Bamboo Wedding" by Sujatha Fernandes first appeared in *Aster(ix) Journal* on MAY 1, 2017.

"What We Know About Men" by Isobel O'Hare first appeared in *Aster(ix) Journal* on NOVEMBER 14, 2017.

"Two Poems" by Rina Garcia Chua first appeared in *Aster(ix) Journal* on MAY 2, 2018.

"Native Tongue" by Ola Osifo Osaze first appeared in *Aster(ix) Journal* on OCTOBER 10, 2018.

"Preferences" by Amina Gautier first appeared in *Aster(ix) Journal* on JULY 20, 2017.

"Lost the Root" by Isabel Acevedo first appeared in *Aster(ix) Journal* on JUNE 18, 2017.

"The World We Choose, the World We Love" by Michelle Yasmine Valladares first appeared in *Aster(ix) Journal* on FEBRUARY 7, 2017.

"Dao Strom in Conversation" by Vi Khi Nao first appeared in *Aster(ix) Journal* on FEBRUARY 18, 2018.

"Powder Puff" by Estella Gonzalez first appeared in *Aster(ix) Journal* on FEBRUARY 18, 2015.

"La Llorona at the Saloon" by José Angel Araguz first appeared in *Aster(ix) Journal* on MARCH 19, 2016.

"The Chemist's Wife" by Em Rose first appeared in *Aster(ix) Journal* on JUNE 9, 2017.

"How to be Courageous: Llanto Mundo" first appeared in *Aster(ix) Journal* on DECEMBER 15, 2017.

"Tal'-s-Go Gal'-Quo-Gi Di-Ded'-Qua-S-Do-Di Tsa-La-Gi Di-Go-Whe-Li / Beginning Cherokee" by Qwo-Li Driskill first appeared in *Aster(ix) Journal* on MAY 12, 2015.

www.ingramcontent.com/pod-product-compliance
Lightning Source LLC
Chambersburg PA
CBHW030628190726
48286CB00008B/2442
* 9 7 8 1 9 4 2 5 4 7 1 0 5 *